Praise for *The Path of Comp*

"For many of us, pastoral counselor Ron Gree. in how to care for those in need in a way that is effective and Christian. In this wonderful book, Ron teaches us how to be more compassionate in a time when that Christian virtue is in short supply among us. *The Path of Compassion* is a gift."

—**William H. Willimon**, best-selling author, Professor of the Practice of Christian Ministry and former Dean of the Chapel at Duke University Divinity School, United Methodist Bishop (retired)

"Drawing on the rich resources of biblical passages and insights from others, along with personal stories and professional encounters, Greer explores with deep insight the meaning and practice of compassion. He takes the reader through the ways in which heart, soul, and mind intersect to bring compassion to life, intellectually, spiritually, emotionally, and practically. *The Path of Compassion* is a significant reflection on a much needed discipline for living in a stressful, complex world."

—**Larry M. Goodpaster**, United Methodist Bishop (retired), Bishop-in-Residence at Candler School of Theology, Emory University, Atlanta

"Weaving stories, scripture, and substantial theological depth throughout *The Path of Compassion*, Ron Greer offers nourishment and wisdom to deepen our faith and strengthen our witness to Christ's presence among us."

—**Jan Love**, Mary Lee Hardin Willard Dean, Candler School of Theology, Emory University

"One cannot read a page of *The Path of Compassion* without at least one 'Aha' moment, a profound lesson in etymology, or outright tears of empathy. The volume is beautifully written. As great as Ron's past works have been, this is his best yet!"

—**Bill Curry**, retired NFL player, head football coach, communicator, educator, motivator, and author

"When your life seems to be coming apart at the seams, you need a wise guide who can skillfully help you pull things back together. I have found Ron Greer to be that wise guide. In *The Path of Compassion*, Ron shows us how to anchor our lives to scripture's twin mandates (love God and love neighbor) and find meaning by living a life of compassion. I wholeheartedly recommend this book to anyone willing to explore what it means to truly love with all your heart, soul, and mind."

—**Bill Britt**, Senior Minister, Peachtree Road
United Methodist Church, Atlanta

THE PATH OF
COMPASSION

LIVING WITH HEART, SOUL, AND MIND

RONALD J. GREER

Abingdon Press / *Nashville*

To those who, by example, have been my mentors in living with compassion and grace.

Contents

Introduction

A lawyer, we read, approached Jesus with a question. "Teacher, which commandment in the law is the greatest?" Jesus answered, "You shall love the Lord your God with all your heart, and with all your soul, and with all your mind." It was straight out of the Shema, recited in Jewish morning and evening prayers. The crowd was nodding in agreement.

Jesus went on. "This is the greatest and first commandment." Still more nods. "And a second is like it." The nodding stopped. What *second* is like it? "'You shall love your neighbor as yourself.' On these two commandments hang all the law and the prophets" (Matthew 22:34-40).

Two tenets of the faith, now forever intertwined.

One is from Deuteronomy, the other from Leviticus. Love of God with love of neighbor. Love of neighbor as an expression of our love of God. Love of neighbor as the language, the voice by which we speak to God of our love. Love of others as a natural response to our love of God.

Love of those around us is elevated from merely good deeds to something sacred, sacramental. We experience God in our compassionate relationships. With those for whom we care, a spiritual synergy is known. "Truly I tell you, just as you did it to one of the least of these who are members of my family, you did it to me," is another way he put it (Matthew 25:40).

Compassion is not just at the heart; it is of the heart.

Yet he says more here than simply love of neighbor. Specifically, it is love of neighbor *as love of self!*

Jesus raises the bar of our compassion, to love our neighbor as instinctively as we care for ourselves. Countless times in our lives we react spontaneously to protect or gratify ourselves. We intuitively take care of ourselves. This love of self comes from the instinctive DNA with which we are born. It is foundational. This is the level to which we are asked to elevate our love of others.

Oh, and one other thing: it is to be real.

We have to mean it. We can't be faking it because we *should* be that loving. As close as is humanly possible, I care about you and your welfare with a similar passion as I care about my own. It is the rare person for whom this idea isn't a radical thought. For most of us, achieving that attitude involves something transformational.

This level of care requires compassion with our *whole being*. As with love of self, it must become foundational. This is not a casual enterprise. The desire to care must come not only from deeply within us but also from every level within us, from all that we are. "With all your heart, and with all your soul, and with all your mind," is how he phrased it.

Heart. Soul. Mind. All united, aligned.

In an earlier writing I focused on integrity. The word comes from the Latin *integer*, which means whole, integrated, complete. With integrity, our purposes, our values, and our attitudes are united in harmony. With all our heart, with all our soul, with all our mind. Each aligned, united, with compassion.

With All Your Heart

Compassion is at the heart of the lives to which each of us is called. Yet compassion is not just *at* the heart; it is *of* the heart.

It springs from a heart moved by the awareness of another's pain. Something within calls us to action. We can do nothing else. We see a need. We have to respond. We have been moved, at times overwhelmed, by compassion. We know that in this moment we are called to something beyond ourselves.

Compassion leads with and comes from the heart. We are touched with empathy by the face of human need. Compassion is the desire to be *with* those who struggle, to be emotionally *in* the effort with them, and to facilitate their way *out* of the pain.

There is a spiritual dimension to each level of compassion. Our hearts are intuitively touched with empathy and moved to action from the *imago Dei*, the image of God—or the "Christ in you," as Paul phrased it—with which we are each created. We are complex creatures with mixed agendas—some not so attractive—but at our center there is a God-given goodness that sincerely cares and wants to help.

With All Your Soul

It is grace that inspires and fuels our compassion

in times of quiet reflection and prayer;
in times of insight, glimpsing the true self God created in us;

in times of inspiration, feeling a call to a purpose greater than ourselves;

in times of being lost, being forgiven, and being welcomed home.

In each of these times, we have known God's grace.

Our response to grace is to live more graciously.

Then sometimes—no, often—we know God's grace with a human face.

At times God speaks with a still, small voice, and at times with a human accent. *When God's grace is seen in another's face, its expression is one of compassion. When it is heard in a human voice, the inflection is one of loving-kindness.* In those moments we know what Jacob felt when he was graciously received by his brother Esau and said to him, "for truly to see your face is like seeing the face of God—since you have received me with such favor" (Genesis 33:10).

Our lives have been touched by just such personal expressions of grace.

In quiet moments of prayer in the early morning or in a friend's thoughtful gesture at just the moment we needed it, our hearts swell or we are moved to tears. We know we have received a gift we did not see coming. It was more meaningful than we ever could have imagined or deserved. We have been blessed. We have received a gift of grace.

Our response to grace is to live more graciously. It is grace that motivates our compassion. When we receive the gift of loving-kindness, we are moved to live, heartfelt, with compassion. But first we are touched. This is where compassion begins. Within the soul. Before we reach out to touch the lives of others, we first are touched. Before we seek to be a blessing, we are blessed.

Another life is then touched. Another soul is blessed. The cycle moves full circle. This is compassion. It is more than a feeling or even an action. It is a process that springs from all of our being. It begins with grace.

With All Your Mind

For this heartfelt, soul-inspired compassion to be engaged into action, intentional choices have to be made. When we think of compassion, usually our focus is on the emotion, the feeling of it. But for compassion to be lived in relationships, decisions have to be made. Action has to be taken. How do we channel this feeling into a living, breathing experience that makes a difference in someone's life? This involves the mind.

I have to think, discern, and decide. Then I have to act. Not just to *feel compassion* but to *be compassionate*. The hallmark of "compassion of the mind" is living out our compassion.

The mind brings wisdom. No matter how deeply we may feel it, there is only so much each of us has to give. Only so much time, energy, availability. So we have to discern and then to decide.

To what do we feel called? By what do we feel inspired? How shall we invest that time? To whom or to what will that energy go? At what point do we need to set boundaries, to pause, to rest and save ourselves to engage another day?

How shall we respond when this warm feeling of compassion encounters the living, breathing needs of the world? How shall we channel our compassion? How shall we translate this emotion into the living of our lives?

Choices must be discerned and action taken. Compassion is, indeed, of the heart, of the soul, *and* of the mind.

Compassion is not just an emotion nor only an inspiration nor simply an action. Compassion is all three working together in beautiful synergy. It involves a feeling of empathy, an experience of grace, and an impassioned engagement. These are the levels of compassion—heart, soul, and mind—and they will be our focus as we bring our *all* to the important calling of compassionate living.

PART I

Compassion of the Heart

CHAPTER 1

"Pretend We're Dancing"

. . . and a time to dance.
—Ecclesiastes 3:4b

He was a young man in his early thirties—bright, busy, developing his career with loads of potential. And his grandmother was dying. She had fought the good fight with cancer through a long and difficult struggle. The ordeal was nearing its end.

Her grandson flew to Virginia to see her. It would be their final visit.

Her pain was severe, and her body was now frail. She always had been a lady of independence and dignity. Her new reality, with its dependency and indignities, was humbling, if not at times humiliating. Bone cancer made walking impossible. She was now reliant on kind hearts and strong arms.

Her joys in life, once abundant, were narrowed to a precious few. Her heart leaped as one of those few— this handsome young grandson—came into her room. They embraced and spent the afternoon together talking and laughing.

The next morning she was scheduled for radia-
tion to help reduce the pain. These would be her final
moments in the sunlight, as she would ride the few
blocks to the clinic. An attendant pushed her wheel-
chair to the driveway. This lady of dignity would have
to be helped even the few steps from the wheelchair
to the car.

Her grandson reached down and wrapped his
arms around her tiny body. He lifted her in the air to
carry her the short distance. His eyes brightened, and
with a lilt in his voice he said, "Gran . . . pretend we're
dancing!"

Compassion springs from that Christlike place within every human heart.

Compassion has the spirit of wanting to bring others into the dance. The word *compassion* means to suffer together. To be compassionate is to offer myself from the heart. It means we care and are willing to be personal. Compassion is about getting involved. About making a difference. Compassion means to get into the ditch willingly with another and patiently, supportively endure the struggle *together*.

Compassion is to be willing to join others who are suffering in the desire to alleviate their pain.

It comes from the Latin *pati*, which has an interesting combination of meanings: to suffer, to endure, and to be patient.[1] The word itself is formed from the Latin "to suffer" (*passion*) "with" (*com*) another. Compassion is to patiently feel the pain with another as we support and bring the aid we can.

Life can be terribly difficult. "Pretend we're dancing!"—or words like them—are ones we need to hear and be lifted by a gracious, generous spirit. *Compassion involves asking another to dance.* The loving invitation comes both from a place of kindness and a desire for connection. To be asked to dance is to be invited into loving relationship by one who wants to join *with* you on the journey.

> Dance, then, wherever you may be;
> I am the Lord of the Dance, said he.
> And I'll lead you all wherever you may be,
> And I'll lead you all in the dance, said he.

> —"Lord of the Dance"

Learning this dance means to live with a loving spirit. As I have come to think of it, this involves four different expressions of care. Each is valuable. Each is important. Each overlap. And each is slightly different from the others. They are:

> Sympathy
>> Empathy
>>> Compassion
>>>> Loving-Kindness

Sympathy Is to Be *With*

The first of these expressions of care is the experience of sympathy. Sympathy is an invitation to dance *with* another. It is to care enough to take the time, energy, and focus to be with someone who does not need to feel alone.

Sympathy is an emotional response of concern at another's misfortune.

Sydney Carter, "Lord of the Dance," copyright © 1963 Stainer & Bell, Ltd. (Admin. Hope Publishing Company, Carol Stream, IL 60188). All rights reserved. Used by permission.

Now stay with me here. Let's get technical for a moment, for this distinction is important.

Presence is when we are humbly sitting with those who are hurting in the midst of what has been done and can't be fixed.

Sympathy is similar in meaning with its linguistic cousin *empathy* but with an important difference. The root of both words is from the Greek *pathos* meaning "suffering." Yet the origin of the first syllable of *sympathy* is from the Greek *sum* meaning "with another" or "together."[2]

To be *sympathetic* is to sincerely care for, to be with, another person in a spirit of concern. It is supportive. It is caring. Sympathy is to be meaningfully present in the other person's life. It is to be *with* the other.

> *Gabe, a young man with a kind heart, was sitting on a park bench with a homeless woman. The woman was eating a hot dog he bought for her from a street vendor. He offered to take her to a restaurant, but she said this would be just fine, thank you. And they talked. After a pause in the conversation, he said to her, "You know, Sally, if I can help with anything you need—" She cut him off in mid-sentence, "I don't want your help!" She said, "I want your company."*

Sympathy highlights the importance of *presence*. For those in pain, there is no greater gift we can offer than to quietly, respectfully be with them. The gift is the gift of yourself. When you are fully present, those who are hurting feel connected and no longer alone.

Presence is when we are not trying to do or fix anything but humbly sitting with them in the midst of what has been done and can't be fixed.

This idea of *presence* is surely a part of what Jesus meant when he said, "For where two or three are gathered in my name, I am there among them" (Matthew 18:20). There is a supportive power felt in the company of one who brings that calming spirit of caring.

Sympathy is not to be confused with *pity*, which implies detachment and often condescension. It seems the understanding of the two words is often blurred, which can shortchange sympathy into nothing more than a Hallmark gesture.

How shall I put it? Pity is simply *recognition* of someone's anguish. There is no heart in it. Pity is an awareness of someone's distress but from a distance. There is no personal caring or desire to be involved. Pity implies the aloofness of the cliché, "There but for the grace of God go I."

Sympathy is much more. Sympathy cares.

When sympathy is felt, the other person matters. It's from the heart. It is—back to the Greek origin—a desire *to be with* another in that person's pain.

Sympathy is akin to the idea of consolation. *Console* comes from the Latin *consolari*—meaning "with solace."[3] As with sympathy, to console is *to be with* another in order to bring comfort and support. Both terms point to the importance of presence. Being with. Showing up. Caring enough to be with someone in the valley of his or her pain is one of the most intimate gifts that can be given. And one of the most courageous.

Sympathy tells those in pain that they are not alone, and that is the exact message those who suffer most need to hear. Indeed, they are not alone.

Sympathy is to be with them in their suffering. Empathy is to be in their suffering with them.

Empathy Is to Be *In*

The next level of caring is *empathy*. As sympathy is being *with* each other, the focus of empathy is on the emotion that springs from *within* the heart of the one who cares, and cares deeply.

We look into the faces of human need, and a voice from deep within resonates and is touched. We feel it. We get it. We understand because we have, in our own way, been there—or close enough—to the distress they are feeling. Thus, knowing what it is like, we are more personally ready to join them in this compassionate dance. The more deeply I connect with myself, the more deeply I can connect with you.

So sympathy is the heartfelt dance *with*, and empathy, even more deeply, comes from the dance *within*.

Again, the word origins illuminate their meanings. The body of each word is from *pathos*, meaning "suffering." Each points to being in the presence of someone in pain. Whereas the *sym* in *sympathy* means "with," the *em* in *empathy* means "in."[4]

The difference is in the type of feeling and engagement. To be *with* those in pain is meaningful and important. But to be *in* the pain with them takes the caring to a new level.

> *Sympathy is to be with them in their suffering.*
> *Empathy is to be in their suffering with them.*

As a pastoral counselor I have the honor of being with persons in pain as they speak of the tenderest and most personal points in their lives. They sit with me and tell their stories. They talk of a relationship betrayed, or
> of a life ended, or
>> of a dream that crashed, or
>>> *of a hope that is slowly fading.*

You know all about this. You, too, have been there countless times as you listen to friends or colleagues. You are just as touched as they describe where they have been and the feelings that go with them still.

> *A friend speaks to us of the love of her life. The fluke meeting at a history lecture. The coffee afterward. The romance that followed as she got to know the man she always longed she would one day find. The marriage. Their children. The fleeting, wonderful years together.*
> *Then the diagnosis. His steep decline.*
> *She speaks slowly of how they attempted to savor every moment while saying goodbye. Fiercely holding on while having to let go.*

We are moved by her tender story. Our focus remains on her, on her life, her marriage, and her loss, but what she has spoken touches us and resonates within us. As she begins her story, she has our full, focused attention. As she takes us through her life's journey, our hearts are moved. We are no longer just *with her*— we are *in the experience* with her.

Empathy involves suffering with another's distress. It begins with what is called "cognitive empathy," the ability to be aware of and understand another person's emotional experience. It means to see out of our own life stories what it must be like for her, as we look into the eyes of someone else and hear her story.

Cognitive empathy is to understand. Then emotional empathy is to join in her struggle and share it with her—to resonate emotionally with what she must be going through. It mirrors her pain. It experiences the hurt vicariously. We feel empathy's Greek origin *empatheia*—*em* ("in") *pathos* ("suffering").[5] As best we can, we enter her life experience. We see through her eyes, from her perspective. Our hearts go out to her.

Compassion wants to make a difference.

Carl Rogers, an educator and psychologist of the twentieth century, wrote, "To sense the [other]'s private world as if it were your own, but without ever losing the 'as if' quality—this is empathy."[6] Empathy never implies a loss of boundaries, losing touch with the reality that it is the other person's dilemma and not our own. Yet it brings a personal understanding, a resonance. We get it. We identify and respond from the heart.

It was one of those moments I knew I would always remember. Our Sunday school class served lunch one Saturday at the Atlanta Day Shelter for Women and Children. We warmed up some lasagna, toasted French bread, and added a salad—then sweet tea from Chick-fil-A.

We were about to serve the food when the director of the shelter took me aside and asked if I would mind saying a blessing before the meal. Of course, I'd be glad to. She picked up a microphone and began giving directions for the lunch. Naturally, I began thinking of what I was going to pray. And suddenly it dawned on me. Standing there, about to say grace, I realized virtually nothing for which I normally thanked God or for which I prayed to God applied to a single one of these homeless families.

Virtually nothing. I remember to this day looking out at that group wondering what on earth I was going to say. There I saw a young mother, a child herself, holding her little baby. The young woman, who looked like a high school sophomore, was staring into the distance—like a frightened deer in the headlights. Homeless, with an infant. I couldn't imagine.

Just in front of me, I looked down into the dark brown eyes of a little girl, no more than three, sitting on her mother's lap. I remember her badly worn sweater. It had faded over the years but once was purple and pink. Buttons missing. Holes. Frayed. We would have been too embarrassed to have donated it to Goodwill. Yet she was wearing it. She was looking up at me—"expectantly" is the best word I know— expectantly listening for what I was about to say. This is one thing we had in common. I was looking forward to hearing what I was going to say, too.

"What on earth is about to come out of my

mouth?" I was still asking myself as I was handed the microphone.

With the grace of God, somehow I got through it. The best I can recall, I prayed for food, shelter, God's nearness, and warmth on a cold winter night. It wasn't pretty, but it was serviceable, and it was over. Thank you, Lord.

I don't quite know how to say this, but I walked back from the dining room to the kitchen . . . changed. It was something about that moment. Having to stand before a group of homeless women and children and put into words a prayer to God, on their behalf, that brought the struggle, the plight of their lives into focus for me like nothing before. To pray that prayer for them with integrity, without trite clichés—for just that instant, I saw life through their lenses.

Northside Drive is the long road in Atlanta that connects our two worlds. Mine is on the north end, and the shelter is on the south. I drove back up Northside that afternoon with a new understanding of the desperation of their lives. I arrived at my end of Northside with an empathy for the desperation of theirs and a new appreciation of the abundance of mine.

I left the shelter filled with women literally fighting for survival. As one of them said to me, fighting "for me and my babies." I finally got it. From that day I continue to have a deeper understanding, a profound gratitude, and the resulting feeling of wanting to give back.

Empathy means others matter to us. We care about them and allow our hearts to become involved in their lives. We then resonate with what they are feeling—whether it is hurt or frustration or fear. We are *in it* with them. As Father Thomas Keating put it, "If one goes to one's own heart, one will find oneself in the heart of everyone else."[7]

Sympathy is the heartfelt awareness of another's struggle.

Empathy is the heartfelt resonance by which we are touched with that person's struggle.

Compassion Is to Make a Difference

There is then the expression of caring we know as compassion. Compassion involves each facet of sympathy and of empathy, *plus the desire to do something about it.* Empathy is to feel someone's pain; compassion is to feel the person's pain *and* to join him or her in addressing it. Compassion wants to respond. Compassion feels another's ache and begins to move into action. In this relational dance, compassion is moving from the invitation to getting on the dance floor.

Remember that the origin of compassion means "to suffer, to endure, and to be patient." To be willing to suffer is the resonance of empathy. Enduring patience is a quality of presence, a hallmark of sympathy. These are cornerstones to compassion. Yet compassion embodies these and adds still another dimension.

The definition of *compassion* in its current usage adds to its original meaning the words, "sympathetic consciousness of others' distress *together with a desire to alleviate it*" (italics mine).[8]

Compassion wants to make a difference.

Sympathy and empathy are essential facets of compassion, but they are its more *passive* elements. With full compassion we are moved emotionally *and* are ready to move intentionally in letting our care be felt.

You feel a mild hunger in midafternoon, and you go to the kitchen and get a banana. It is a natural response. You hardly give it a thought. Likewise, someone within your awareness feels a different need. You realize that this is your friend's first Mother's Day since her mom died. You reach for the phone to make a call or for a pen to write a note, just as naturally as you would have walked to the kitchen for your own need. Compassion in its fullness becomes natural, intuitive. We continue to love ourselves. We simply grow to include our neighbors with a similar instinctive grace.

I have heard several use the identical phrase when describing a decision made involving some caring sacrifice. "I can't *not* do it," is how they put it. With compassion, the empathy wells up within us, and we have to act. We "can't *not* do it."

Compassion comes from a deeply felt place of the heart. It is far more than simply doing good deeds. It isn't out for any recognition. It doesn't want a merit badge. It isn't about ego. In fact, compassion is hardly aware of itself. It becomes a natural response—you can do no other. You can't not do it. It is intuitively to "love your neighbor as yourself."

A Spirit of Loving-Kindness

At the heart of compassion is *loving-kindness*. Simply put, loving-kindness means we not only want others to be free of hurt, but we want for them lives of meaning and joy. It points to a generosity of spirit in wanting the most fulfilled lives for those around us and a willingness to join them in making that happen.

As author Frederick Buechner put it, compassion "is the knowledge that there can never really be any peace and joy for me until there is peace and joy finally for you too."[9]

If my attitude toward life and its relationships isn't loving, then I've missed the relational starting point of my faith.

When we are compassionate, we look into a person's eyes and want his or her life to be filled with the same joy we seek for ourselves. Our empathy sparks that emotional response within us, and our loving-kindness then inspires us to act on it in ways that matter to those beyond us.

In Jesus's beautiful economy of words, he summarized the heart of his message. Love of God. Love of neighbor as self. Those are the fundamentals. That is what we are about as followers of his. In our response to our love of God, we promote "love of neighbor" as closely as we can to a parallel with "love of self." I am to respond to my neighbor as instinctively and lovingly as I would to myself.

Again. Love of God. Love of neighbor as self. But Jesus's teaching didn't stop there. He then gave this message his grand finale as he added, "On these two commandments hang all the law and the prophets" (Matthew 22:40). There is his exclamation point! This final statement puts *love of God and neighbor* in its proper place—at the center of our faith.

All of the law, all of the teachings, all of our values are to be seen through the lenses of love of God and neighbor.

Loving-kindness, then, is at the heart of living out a Christian life. Love of God and neighbor come first. As Christians, how we relate with God, with neighbor, and with all of humankind begins with love.

If my attitude toward life and its relationships isn't loving, then I've missed the relational starting point of my faith.

Everything . . . everything in the law and the prophets hangs on these two directives. Love is the primary value and priority on which our lives are to be based. Love is where we begin and end. The Alpha and Omega.

Paul would later underscore the same lesson in his writing: "And now faith, hope, and love abide, these three; and the greatest of these is love" (1 Corinthians 13:13). It doesn't get any bigger than that. Faith and hope are some impressive company. But the most important of the three is love. In any context, love is our default position. It is to be the core intent. Any and every other value—no matter how honorable—has to take a back seat to loving compassion. Everything hangs on these two commandments.

In an earlier writing I had done on integrity, I emphasized the importance of being grounded in healthy values since living in this world can get complex and confusing. Decisions we make on the paths we are to take are not always obvious—especially when two worthwhile values are competing with each other.

"Dueling values" is what I tend to call these. It's when a decision has to be made between two paths, the classic fork in the road, and both choices are honorable. The reason to take each path is based on a solid value, but I can't take both. Either–or. One or the other. Resulting in dueling values.

The classic example is when the man with the withered hand came to Jesus to be healed on the Sabbath, when no work was to be done. Jesus knew this could well be the only time their paths would cross. The man was to be healed now or never. It was a choice between honoring the Jewish teaching of no labor on the Sabbath or honoring his compassionate loving-kindness (Luke 6:6-11).

Love won.

The life and teachings of Jesus Christ consistently remind us that whenever a choice was to be made between loving compassion and any other value, love always won. It was a given.

Love always wins.

Love is to be our top and overriding priority. As persons of faith, it is what our lives are to be about.

So why is love so important to our faith? Because, as John wrote, "God is love" (1 John 4:8, 16). Love is the essential spirit of God. Love is God's essence. And time after time the Scriptures point us back to our essence as those who have been created in God's image. They remind us of "the Christ in you" or of our "original blessing."[10] How fully we have lived from that spiritual core, from the Christ in us, is seen in the depth of our love in the lives we have touched.

I have a friend who is a physician in South Carolina. His name is John. He is retired from his practice and consults with hospitals in the region. One morning an oncologist invited John to join him for rounds with his residents. They went into the room of a woman who had been diagnosed with an aggressive form of cancer. The doctor and his residents did what they do in describing the diagnosis, the prognosis, upcoming treatment, then the back and forth with questions.

Throughout all of this, this dear woman, feeling so terribly awkward and exposed, was nervously fidgeting and wringing her hands. Finally, they were finished, and as they were about to leave her room the physician asked John if he would like to add anything. He stepped up to the side of her bed, looked at her with the kindest eyes, and said, "Christina, you have the busiest hands I've ever seen. May I hold them?"

There, in front of God and everybody, this doctor she had never laid eyes on sat on the edge of her bed and held her hands. There they talked like old friends as if there were no one else in the room. They talked about her cancer, the treatment, playfully talked about her upcoming wig, and even where she went to church. As the conversation concluded, he patted her hands, said goodbye, and they all left her room.

The following day, as she was about to be discharged, her physician came by to see her. He said he hoped she had been treated well during her stay. She assured him she had, listing all those who had been so kind.

Then she added, "You know, that doctor who came with you yesterday? When he sat on my bed, held my hands, and we talked, that's when I knew I could deal with this."

John was later to add, "She wasn't healed, but she was made whole."

In your love and compassion with those you meet, you, too, in your own way, will take their hands. Though their struggles will not disappear, your loving-kindness will touch their hearts, and by the grace of God, they will be made whole.

CHAPTER 2

To Look from the Heart

"If your eye is healthy, your whole body is full of light."
—Luke 11:34

Compassion begins with seeing.

There is an intentional vision that compassion requires. *It means we look from a place in our hearts that cares to a place in our neighbor's heart that matters.* Compassion means that I look through the veneer, the ways others may be alike or different, and focus on the heart of the one who is before me. If I look from the heart, I begin to *see*. I begin to see you and all of humankind as important, worthy, and unique.

Compassion requires that I be in the moment. Present. Available. And it always requires that I care. If I am in relationship with you, I really want to know who you are. If we are passing acquaintances, I want to connect in a meaningful way in the moments we share together. Cultivated compassion becomes who we are. We care. Others matter. We pause to look. And then we see.

This desire involves our idea of sympathy. We are willing to get outside of ourselves—our agenda, our focus, our needs—

and be *with* others in theirs. To look from the heart is to join with them, sympathetically, in their life stories.

I was listening to a friend tell one of his delightful tales. He can tell a great story. Usually I'm enthralled by them, but this time I never got past the first sentence. I haven't a clue what he said after that. He had begun with the words, "I was talking with John, the man at the cleaners the other day. . . ." That was as far as I got.

It was such a simple statement, but I was stunned by it. You see, I stop by my cleaners at least once a week, and a gracious woman always helps me. I realized that not only had I not had a meaningful conversation with her but I also didn't even know her name. I had been, I hope, kind and courteous to her, but I had never gotten to know her. I didn't hear another word my friend said. The only thought on my mind was, *I don't even know her name.*

> *The Gospel of Mark (8:22-26) contains a vivid story. "Can you see anything?" Jesus asked the blind man who stood before him. He and his disciples had just landed on the northern coast of the Sea of Galilee. They were hardly off the boat, their robes still wet from wading ashore, when a group of townspeople, leading a man who was blind, began making their way to Jesus. Mark wrote that they "begged [Jesus] to touch him."*
>
> *Jesus took this blind man by the hand and led him away from the crowd. Just as Jesus took his blindness seriously, he took the man personally. This intimate moment of healing was not a public event. The stranger's eyes and his soul were about to be touched. Then, facing the man, he put saliva on each of his eyes and*

touched them. At this time in human history hygiene was, at best, crude. To heal the man's eyes, Jesus had to get to them. With the moisture of his own saliva he wiped away the grime and dust that had collected. With the tips of his fingers he then gently touched the man's eyes and the miracle began.

"Can you see anything?" he asked. It had been years since this man had opened his eyes to see, and he squinted from the newfound glare of the sun. What he said was so interesting. "[Yes,] I can see people, but they look like trees, walking." They look like trees. This was the only healing in which Jesus ever participated that took place in two steps. He touched the man the first time and, yes, he could see—he could see people—but they looked like . . . well, trees. Not like persons. Trees, objects, things.

With each reading of this Scripture I instinctively pause at this point. How much—how much of my life is lived out with the vision of only the first touch, seeing persons as trees walking? It may well include being courteous and considerate. Even showing acts of caring but *not being personal.*

To look *is one thing. The vision of the second touch is to* see.

I had always been kind to the person with whom I spoke at the cleaners. But I didn't even know her name. Seeing persons as trees, objects, walking in our midst.

How many marriages have partners looking across the breakfast table at someone each of them hardly knows, at someone he or she has hardly tried to know? Trees walking.

How many parents are yelling from the sidelines for their sons and daughters to live out the unfulfilled dreams of their own youth? They are rooting for themselves, of course. Trees walking.

Those who live with the vision of the first touch may know the character value of compassion, but it is from a respectful distance, caring without being personal. With the vision of the first touch, it is still too much about us. Perhaps the motivation is too much about ego—to maintain a caring self-image or to foster a reputation for compassion. The vision of the first touch brings the potential for a diluted sympathy, with a detached brand of kindness. But more is required if one is to feel full *sympathy* or true *empathy*, much less the fullness of *compassion*.

The Second Touch

Then Jesus lifted his hands and touched the man's eyes a second time, and, as Mark writes, the man "looked intently and his sight was restored, and he saw everything clearly." (v. 25)

The vision of the second touch is to come more closely to seeing each other as God sees. It is to see from the heart. It is life changing. We see differently. In the language of the faith, *the parallel of being "born again" is to be "touched again."*

To *look* is one thing. The vision of the second touch is to *see*. The vision of the second touch
    is seeing with clarity,

is seeing from a heart that truly cares,
is looking, not at trees, but to persons.

It means looking into their eyes with feeling and warmth and understanding.

The vision of the second touch is to see with empathy and to want to respond with compassion. Author Frederick Buechner wrote, "If we are to love our neighbors, before doing anything else we must see our neighbors . . . we must see not just their faces but the life behind and within their faces."[1]

> We flew into the airport in Istanbul on a Sunday afternoon in October. It was a cloudless day, and a driver was taking us to our hotel. As we rode near the Bosphorus Strait there was a beautiful city park with families scattered over it on their blankets. I commented, "What a great way to enjoy a Sunday afternoon—a family picnic in the park." There was silence in the van. "Mr. Greer," our driver said, "they aren't having picnics. Those are refugee families from Syria. The park is where they live."
>
> I looked again. Those weren't just blankets. Some were makeshift tents. They weren't picnic baskets. They were all their earthly belongings.

Compassion changes how we see humankind. We go from *looking* to *seeing*. Intentionality is required. It means looking into the eyes of the other person with the sensitivity and respect that person and my relationship with him deserves. And as I look through different eyes, I speak with a different voice. We will not be getting to know every clerk's life story, but he will know he has been addressed as the person of dignity he is.

Jesus touched the man's eyes a second time. And now he saw everything clearly.

I know of a couple who would ask one of their children on the way home from any restaurant—and it was always a surprise who would be called on—the simple question, "What color?" The children knew what their parents meant. What color were the eyes of their server at dinner? The point of the question is that their waitpersons are men and women of dignity and worth. When you speak to them they deserve to be addressed respectfully. Respect is shown not by looking down at the menu and mumbling our orders but by looking the servers in the eye and speaking with the regard they deserve.

"What color?" For they are not trees walking.

> The man who picks up our garbage twice a week was running early. It was two days before Christmas, and we had a cash gift for him. I was going to tape the envelope to the trash can but had not expected him until later.
>
> I rushed downstairs, grabbed the money, and dashed to the driveway. Our sacks of garbage had just landed in the back of his truck, and he was climbing into the cab. I jogged to catch him before he pulled away. "Here is a little something for Christmas, and thank you for all that you do. I hope you have a Merry Christmas."
>
> We introduced ourselves and shook hands. Vic thanked me and apologized for getting my hand wet and dirty.
>
> Walking back to the house I thought, Wet and dirty was so much better.
>
> No more taping an envelope to the garbage can. I

want to speak to Vic. I want to see his eyes and shake his hand.

Me and My Shadow

There can be a darker side to the limited vision of only the first touch. It can make us vulnerable to distancing and even polarizing.

As we look through the eyes of the first touch we can find ways to diminish others who are perceived as different. We can see as lesser those we sense not to be "like me." As we desensitize, we dehumanize—some even demonize. They are put down and given slang names to depersonalize them. It becomes "us" versus "them."

Someone who doesn't agree with us becomes something less in our eyes, inferior, if not a total idiot. Seeing people as trees, things. This is seeing them as less than human beings created in God's image, with the same feelings, needs, and aspirations as the rest of us. Trees. Things.

The motivation for this distortion comes from various origins. We may want to bring others down to elevate ourselves by comparison. This is usually grounded in personal insecurities and fears tucked away in our subconscious.

Swiss psychiatrist Carl Jung referred to this as our "shadow," containing our fears of who we are—our weaknesses, our pettiness, our self-centeredness, all the ways we may be in contradiction to our own aspirations. These fears lurk in the darkness, in the shadows outside our conscious awareness. It is the part of ourselves with which we are displeased or even ashamed of and have not allowed into the light of day.

Since we have never acknowledged these parts of ourselves—
*since we have never seen them within ourselves—we can only
"see" them in others*. It's called "projection." It is when we project the fears and inferiorities and insecurities we secretly have
about who we are onto others. The hypocrite is readily judgmental of those who seem hypocritical. The gossip puts down
those who are "always talking about other people."

We objectify them and critically see them as "trees walking."
We do not allow ourselves to see them as the persons they are
with strengths and weaknesses, for we have projected onto them
parts of ourselves we most dislike. We reject them for what we
don't care for in us.

This is the truth to which Jesus was pointing when he spoke
of our looking past the log in our own eyes to point out the
speck in someone else's. This is the basis of most prejudice. The
ways we put others down tend to be the exact ways, in our heart
of hearts, we fear is true of us.

To the degree I am high and mighty in my criticism of someone's arrogance—yes, to that same degree—I have not yet come
to terms with my own arrogance, or at least the insecurity that
hides behind it. I resent in other persons what I subconsciously
see in me. It is much simpler to pull out my prejudice and slam
others than it is to address the real problem or fear in my own
life.

They become the "enemy" to whom Jesus referred as he
encouraged us to *love* our enemies (Matthew 5:44; Luke 6:27,
35). I believe he was inviting us to befriend those denied parts of
our own hearts that this external enemy represents.

Through intentional self-exploration, I need to get to know
the attitudes and feelings tucked away and hidden in my subconscious that give rise to my prejudice and push others away.

I need to look at these distasteful parts of myself and either bless them or address them. Some can be addressed or at least partially resolved. They may come from old wounds that have left us emotionally limping or from childhood experiences that have negatively distorted who we see in the mirror. Then there are other parts of ourselves, such as weaknesses and disabilities that came with our DNA, we must learn successfully to accept. We must come to terms with these or they will haunt us the rest of our lives.

Bless them or address them.

As I have accepted or addressed those lesser-desired parts of me, then I will lessen my tendency to see my neighbors through those judgmental lenses. I can see them, with their strengths and weaknesses, for the fellow sojourners they are.

Fred Rogers, of *Mister Rogers* fame, is said to have carried in his wallet a note that read, "Frankly, there isn't anyone you couldn't learn to love once you heard their story." We hear our neighbors' stories, and we come to see them, without judgment, as the brothers and sisters they are.

Then, and only then, are we ready to get to know our neighbors for who they really are.

"Do to others as <u>they</u> would have you do to them."

The clarity of the second touch encourages me to move beyond my projections and my prejudice and increasingly brings into focus the reality and the beauty of who each child of God really is. I then see the best in people. My tendency to judge is lessened. Jesus couldn't have expressed it more bluntly, "Do not judge" (Matthew 7:1). In judgment's place is acceptance. In place of judgment is respect, a desire to know others' life stories, and an acceptance of who they are.

Respect is relating to others with thoughtfulness and regard for their feelings. Respect is treating them with dignity and consideration. We stand side by side as sisters and brothers together. As peers. No one better than anyone else.

This shift to the second touch is essential if my life is to embody a meaningful measure of compassion and loving-kindness. However I chose to deal with my personal feelings of inadequacy or inferiority, I must get "me" out of the way, so I can see you for the unique individual God created in you.

The Second Touch
with Those Who Matter Most

The second touch changes how we see humankind. Strangers look less strange. They seem more like us. The potential for those relationships is then altered by the shift in my vision, in my perspective.

The power of the second touch also transforms the relationships of those who already matter to us. In virtually every marriage with which I work professionally there are two spouses who want their partners to hear them—to hear their desires and needs that are usually understandable, appropriate, and healthy. They each want to be heard, to be taken seriously, and to have the validity of what they are sharing honored. But both are talking, and neither is listening.

Whenever I make it all about me in any relationship, whenever I am focused solely on my needs, I treat the other person as an object. I am not engaged. I am not connecting in the relationship. I am looking at my spouse or my friend as someone to focus on me. He or she is there to meet my needs. A tree, walking.

I may talk and talk about a difficult meeting I had and how I didn't feel heard or my ideas appreciated. Never once even asking, "So how did your luncheon go?" Or perhaps I do but just as a gesture to get it out of the way so we can get back to me. How does the line go from the narcissistic Hollywood movie director at a dinner party? "Enough talk about me. Let's talk about you. What did you think of my latest movie?"

It's all about the sight gained with the second touch. With it, those who matter to us *really* matter to us. We think about them. We want to know them. We want to keep up with them. We want to know how their day is going, what matters to them, what are the joys in their lives. The sorrows. The struggles. We ask about them not to be social or sound gracious—we ask because we really want to know. The sight gained from the second touch transforms us out of ourselves and truly into relationship.

As we engage with acquaintances and in casual relationships, the Golden Rule—"Do to others as you would have them do to you" (Luke 6:31 NAB)—is an excellent North Star that guides our thinking. It is a pillar of compassion. We may not nail exactly what others need, but it will get us in the ballpark. Yet, when it comes to personal relationships, especially those as close as marriage, it isn't personal enough.

Let's say a husband grew up with three brothers. His childhood home was practically a guy's locker room. The language was rough and blunt. His poor mom struggled to encourage any hint of civility or respect among all these males in her home. Now he is married. His communication is blunt, unvarnished, and often crude.

Now let's imagine he is married to a woman from a more refined background who values respect, graciousness, and sensitivity. If he follows the Golden Rule—doing to her as he would have her do to him—he will be offending her night and day. "The Platinum Rule" is the name given to a new directive:

"Do to others as <u>they</u> would have you do to them."

With the vision of the second touch, my perspective is transformed and I see my wife as the person she is. Her needs and wants come into focus, and she becomes my priority. I see her differently. To paraphrase the classic line from Jack Nicholson in the movie *As Good as It Gets*, the power of the second touch "makes me want to be a better man."

My goal in my marriage, at which I fail too often, is for Karen's happiness to be as important to me as my own. This is not exactly a revolutionary new concept. It is precisely what Jesus implored us to do in the other great commandment: "Love your neighbor as yourself."

Here's the irony: as I get out of myself and focus on her instead of me, as I consciously, intentionally love her and meet her needs the best I can—surprise, surprise!—she feels a heartfelt motivation to love me and meet mine. And what do you have then? The foundation of a marriage. Or in another personal relationship with parallel dynamics at work, what you have is a precious friendship. What you have is a truly beautiful thing.

With the grace of the second touch, life is filled with just such blessings. With the grace of the second touch, we see with clarity the beauty of the souls around us. With the grace of the second touch, we are ready to relate with compassion. We celebrate with their joys; we grieve with their sorrows. We see our kinship as never before.

By the way, her name is Henny. My friend at the cleaners. Henny is from Indonesia. If there is anything you'd like to know about her thirteen-year-old daughter or her son who is a senior in high school looking for a college scholarship, or her mom or her sister or her six-year-old nephew who still live in Indonesia, you just let me know. And if you ever hear her talk about the joy of her family's visit to the United States—especially the part about taking that little nephew to Disney World—it will warm your heart and mist your eyes.

CHAPTER 3

To Feel from the Heart

"Jesus wept."
—John 11:35 (KJV)

Yes, compassion begins with seeing. We see beyond ourselves. We begin with a desire to understand, to know what others' lives are about. Then, as they begin to share their stories, we feel something. A resonance. Their stories, their lives, their emotions stir something in us. Our hearts are moved. We are touched. It's called empathy.

One of Dutch master Johannes Vermeer's most admired paintings is Woman in Blue Reading a Letter. This seventeenth-century painting that hangs in the Rijksmuseum in Amsterdam is one that instantly invites us into the story. It shows a woman in a satin blue jacket standing beside her kitchen table intently reading a letter. The first page of the letter rests on the table as she eagerly finishes the next page.

Questions immediately come to mind upon seeing this painting. From whom is the letter? What is it about? What has her so captivated? Look at her face. It is intent but relaxed. There isn't the tension of someone receiving disturbing news. Her mouth hangs slightly open as we do when we are caught up in the moment. There may even be the slightest hint of a smile on her lips.

She may be catching up on the events of the life of someone who clearly matters to her. But who? And about what? Our imaginations take over.

We see the map on the wall behind her that has been transformed into a work of art for the home. Perhaps her husband is a sailor at sea and mailed her this letter from a distant port. The woman in the painting may be pregnant, so we imagine him expressing his love and his eagerness to return home before the baby is due. He may be expressing how hard it is to focus on his job when his thoughts are always of her and longing to be with her.

Or perhaps the letter is from her mother in another city writing of an upcoming family event and hoping she can attend. Maybe her nephew, her sister's son, was just in a school play, and her mom is sharing the highlights of this young actor's exceptional performance. He forgot a line in the second act, paused briefly, and then improvised like a veteran of the stage. The audience never knew of the faux pas.

The letter. The intent look. The faint smile. They ignite our imaginations. We take the bits of information we are given and creatively run with them. Our minds take over and intuitively write the backstory of the painting.

Vermeer never spoke of the real story behind the painting of the woman in blue—if, indeed, she was an actual person—so our imaginations are not distracted.

We are free to look at the painting of this woman,
feel what we feel, and go wherever our imaginations
take us.[1]

The word *empathy* originated in the world of art. The term
was first used in the English language early in the twentieth century, but its origin is from the German *einfühlung*, which meant
"feeling into." The earliest use of the word was in the field of art
to describe the dynamic we feel as we are moved by art in any of
its forms.[2] What we feel as we take in the painting or the performance is our empathetic response. There is a resonance within
to what we see or hear from without. It is our feeling of what
the art stimulates, which we then project onto the work. This
creative moment generates the meaning the painting has for us.[3]

If you hurt, I hurt.
If you struggle, I struggle.

Philosopher Theodore Lipps was another early user of the
term as he applied it to stage performances. He illustrated
empathy as the connection between a viewer in the audience
and a high-wire walker. As the walker steps onto the wire there
is tension throughout the crowd, and then with any sudden jerk
there is a gasp—as if each audience member were on that wire
with him. Lipps wrote, "I feel myself inside of him."[4]

British psychologist Edward Titchener incorporated this
understanding of *einfühlung* into our English "empathy" in
1909.[5] Through the first half of the century, the term *empathy*
began to be applied to human relationships. It was only after

World War II that the field of psychology began to use the word consistently to refer to how we relate to each other.

As someone tells her story, a feeling arises within me. It is a resonance that, in all likelihood, is similar to what she is feeling. As we bring comfort to those who are struggling, our empathy comes from that place deep within us. Though we can never know just how they are feeling, we resonate personally in our hearts and in our memories from our parallel experiences. This connects us with our emotional depth from which we appreciate something of what they must be feeling. It gives us the inspiration to care, as we intuitively engage with the compassion we needed when we were in a similar place.

Karen and I lost our two-year-old son, Eric, in an accident in the early eighties. In my counseling ministry, I see a significant number of grieving parents who are seeking help from someone who knows what that experience is like. At some point in the first counseling session many will say to me, "I wanted to see a counselor who has been there." Some will add, "I could only talk with someone who gets it." They rarely use the word *empathy*, but that is precisely what they mean. They want to open up this heartache only to someone who knows personally the depth and severity of the pain.

For most of life's hurts it is not required that we have the experience of those we comfort. What is required is that we have been to deep emotional and spiritual places and have returned with an awareness of the experience never to be lost.

In this understanding of compassion, we are sisters and brothers in this together, looking out for each other. If you hurt, I hurt. If you struggle, I struggle. G. K. Chesterton said it well, "We men and women are all in the same boat, upon a stormy sea. We owe to each other a terrible and tragic loyalty."[6]

Early in his life, as a circuit-riding lawyer, Abraham Lincoln had become good friends with William McCullough of Bloomington, Illinois. McCullough was the sheriff, and later the county clerk of court.

Years later, as president, Lincoln allowed his friend to volunteer in the Union Army though he was now fifty, had lost sight in one eye, and had an arm severed by a thrasher. Outnumbered at Coffeeville, McCullough rallied his troops, with the reins of his horse in his teeth, riding up and down the battle lines with his saber in his hand. It was there he died.

Word later came to Lincoln that McCullough's daughter, Fanny, was traumatized in her grief over his death. Her moods would swing from violent grief to utter silence. It was reported that those near to her feared "for her consequences."

This stirred something in President Lincoln. He wrote her a tender letter of condolence—something he did only a handful of times. We can only imagine what he was feeling, yet we have some hints. Lincoln had watched his mother die when he was only nine. Then, early in 1862, he and his wife lost their eleven-year-old son, Willie. What followed was a time of darkest grief for him and an emotional breakdown for Mary Todd Lincoln.

The news of his friend's death, followed by the report of Fanny's struggle, touched something deep within this man's heart. He wrote, "In this sad world of ours, sorrow comes to all; and to the young, it comes with bitterest agony, because it takes them unawares. The older have learned to ever expect it."

The wisdom of his counsel continued, "You are

sure to be happy again. The memory of your dear
Father, instead of an agony, will yet be a sad sweet
feeling in your heart, of a purer, and holier sort than
you have known before."[7]

The empathetic resonance with another's pain is essential to the full experience of compassion. I *join* you in this vicarious experience. I don't know exactly how you feel, but if I am fully present with you, I *do* have a heartfelt intuitive sense of my version of your emotions. I can't quite "feel your pain," as the cliché goes, but I can join you in it as I feel my corresponding ache for you. I hurt with you as you hurt.

"Jesus wept." We all remember that classic verse from John 11:35, if only because it is the shortest verse in the Bible.

Jesus had been implored by Lazarus's sisters to come to their home urgently. Their brother and Jesus's friend had died. They were heartbroken as Jesus walked in. It was likely as they embraced that "Jesus wept."

But why? The Scriptures tell us Jesus already knew that Lazarus would recover. So why did he cry with the others? Empathy. Heartfelt empathy. It did not matter that Jesus knew his friend would soon rise up and begin his recovery. Lazarus's sisters were in pain. He resonated with them. He joined them in their pain. That is empathy. From the depths of his heart. Mary and Martha knew they were not alone.

Again, when I think of the original use of the word *empathy* and its association with art, I am reminded that empathy is *our* emotional response. If it springs from appreciating a painting, it comes from how the art speaks to each of us. We then project our meaning onto the work.

We see that clearly when we are in conversation with a group on how we felt about a movie or a concert we had all heard. Our group may be all over the map with how we felt and what we thought. There is a response *from* each of us that is unique *to* each of us. My response and my meaning may or may not correspond that closely to the performer or the screenwriter or the artist's intention.

What we feel is what the artist has inspired within each of our hearts.

If I sit with you and listen to the hurt of your experience, my empathy draws me to you. The heartfelt resonance I feel allows me to accompany you more personally. Empathy connects us.

Yet, I must remember to be cautious not to project my feelings or thoughts or hunches from my heart onto yours. I may project onto a piece of art but not onto someone about whom I care. No matter how powerful the resonance within me is to your story, it is, after all, *your* story—and how I feel may not be just how you are feeling. Thus, I must never assume. I must remember to ask.

And then to listen. Attentively listen.

> *I stumble upon most of my life's meaningful moments. Years ago, I was talking with a woman to whom I had been introduced at church. To our surprise we discovered we had grown up only a few miles from each other in neighboring parishes in Louisiana.*
>
> *Naturally, there was much in common. We were children of the fifties. We had been in each other's hometowns. We knew the landmarks. We felt like kindred spirits with a common bond.*
>
> *We had traveled the same roads. One of us happened to mention we had frequently made the four-*

hour trek to Baton Rouge as a child with our family. It was something else we had in common. Most of my trips were to LSU football games or the family going with my dad on business. A highlight of the trip was the stop at Lea's Restaurant outside Alexandria for Mr. Lea's famous ham sandwiches and pecan pies. Good memories.

Her family trips across our state were different. So different. She was visiting family in Baton Rouge. Prior to the trip, her family packed not only their clothes but all the food they would need between home and her grandmother's. They would not be stopping for anything but gas. (On longer trips, she said, it was known in the community the few places it would be safe to stop for food.)

She is black. I am white.

She told me of a time when she was riding on that two-lane road, which to me was so familiar and felt so safe. Her dad suddenly yelled to the family to "get down, and don't move!" A group of white teenage boys, half drunk, had pulled their car up beside them. The boys were yelling racial profanities. Her dad feared they would run him off the road. He feared for his family. He looked straight ahead and kept driving.

Fortunately, a truck came from the opposite direction, and the carload of punks sped away. Her father said they were gone but to stay down—they might come back. They didn't.

Those few terrifying minutes had lasted an eternity for her, she said. Then this kind woman was silent, looking down. Her eyes welled, as did mine.

I learned we hadn't traveled the same roads at all.

Black and white. Neighboring towns, but two completely different stories from two completely different worlds.

My empathy sparks a resonance from your life experience and mine. But to connect with you, empathy must team with wisdom in not assuming our experiences are the same. So we talk. I get to know you. Our relationship is enriched, and we connect in personal and meaningful ways.

CHAPTER 4

To Listen for the Heart

"Let anyone with ears to hear listen!"
—Mark 4:9

Compassion begins with seeing and feeling. Then hearing. The primary need of those who suffer is not complicated. They need to be heard.

They need someone caring enough to visit,
courageous enough to ask how they are feeling,
and wise enough to be quiet and listen.

It's not what they heard,
it's that they were heard.

Those moments can be sacramental.

Countless times those who have been through one of life's heartaches have spoken to me of how touched they were by the compassion of someone who truly cared. "I couldn't have made it without them," is how it is often said. But rarely do they quote anything that was spoken. If something profound was said, that was not what touched them.

It's not what they heard, it's that they were *heard.*

The moment had more to do with their friend's presence and willingness to listen. Someone cared enough to be with them and hear them talk and talk about what they had been all but bursting to say.

That you listened is far more important than anything you could say.

To be heard is one of the most personal ways of being loved. Remember the last time you thought or even said, "I really felt heard." You knew you had received a gift.

David Augsburger said it beautifully, "Being heard is so close to being loved that for the average person they are almost indistinguishable."[1]

To those who want to care for people who have suffered a heartache, I have often said:

> If you don't know them well, send them a card.
> If you know them moderately well, take them anything from your favorite bakery.
> If you know them well, go by to see them, and give them a hug.
> If you know them really well, pull up a chair, ask them how they are doing, and plan to stay awhile.

Those who are struggling need you to invite them to open up, to create a safe place where they feel your interest and your care. They need to hear, "How are you doing?" from someone who really wants to know. Simple, sincere invitations into relationship from one who will patiently listen can transform the moment from feeling alone to being loved. The finest way to show your love and help them heal is to ask and then listen. (Or as I have heard it said more bluntly, "Show up and shut up.")

The litmus test for a meaningful visit with those who are hurting is this: When the time together was over, did you get with them where they are instead of trying to get them where you wanted them to be?

Quiet is too rarely given its due. The Scriptures guide us: "Oh that you would keep silent, / and it would be your wisdom" (Job 13:5 ESV). Then as James wrote in his epistle, "Let everyone be quick to listen, slow to speak" (1:19).

Humorist Will Rogers, of course, puts it more directly, "Never miss a good chance to shut up."

Yet that is often not the way we live. Excellence in listening is not a skill to which many aspire. To feel truly heard is often the exception and not the rule.

"To cause an avalanche you can shake a mountain or find the right place to drop a snowflake."

Ours is a social-media world in which the theme is to promote me and my brand. *My* photos, *my* activities, *my* life are supposed to be the point. Social media encourages a world in which everyone is talking and few are listening. Mystery writer Margaret Millar was painfully accurate when she said, "Most conversations are simply monologues delivered in the presence of a witness."

Then . . . there is truly listening. This is an active experience. We are not just shutting up. Listening involves focus and concentration. Though we are silent, we are hardly withdrawing in the sense of disengaging. In fact, it is quite the opposite of passivity. We are completely engaged. By our silence, we are simply creating the space that invites them to open up and tell us their story.

As we quietly listen, we connect in ways that can be nothing less than transforming. We aren't distracted. We aren't thinking about something else we need to be doing. We are fully present and completely attentive. Those are moments that touch the heart.

That is *the sacred silence of listening*—as we respond from the heart to the heart. Those times are incarnational moments of God's grace.

A common feeling to any valley we have to travel is the sense of being alone. We ache for company, to be invited out of our isolation. When we are heard—genuinely heard—the aloneness is gone. The isolation vanishes. In the transformation, a caring relationship has taken its place.

I once heard it said, "To cause an avalanche you can shake a mountain or find the right place to drop a snowflake." These intimate, meaningful moments—quiet as a snowflake—can be powerful, even transformative to the one who longs to be heard. No gift is more valuable, especially at those profound points in life, than being heard, understood, and accepted.

The Importance of Listening

One half of all communication is listening. But the attention is consistently on what we *say* and how we *say* it.

We are not listening to achieve our goals or even meet our needs but to help our friend who is in pain meet hers. We want her to heal. We want her to be loved. Being heard is a vital part of the healing and then growing.

The topic is listening—or more precisely, *being heard*—but the real subject is relating, connecting, and caring. Listening is vital to that happening. It means to get outside myself and all my thoughts and concerns and plans. I need to get outside what is important to me and listen, because you are important to me. French philosopher Simone Weil put it so well, "Attention is the rarest and purest form of generosity."[2]

Being heard is often underrated because few understand the reasons for its importance. There are several, and they are unspeakably valuable.

The value of being in relationship. Listening is to make connection. Those who are struggling are working through an issue—perhaps the loss of a job, a dream, or someone they love—an issue they ultimately have to work through within themselves. It is a lonely job. Your invitation for them to open up, into relationship, is your gift. Your listening to them is a reminder that they are not alone as they engage in this lonely task.

I can't love someone I don't know, and I can't know someone to whom I haven't listened.

Being understood. To have someone "get us," when something we feel is important, is of enormous value. The result is an acceptance that confirms the validity of how we feel and even who we are.

> *Psychologist and author Mary Pipher tells about her middle-aged cousin Paul. He is kind. He tries to be*

helpful. He takes care of his disabled mother. He has extended himself countless times—to save a drowning man, to stop a family embroiled in domestic violence.

Paul is a good man. And he has a mental illness. He will periodically have a psychotic breakdown. This leaves him terribly vulnerable and often homeless. Horrifically painful events have happened to Paul during these episodes.

In a rural area of Arkansas, he was arrested while psychotic. The local police had failed to read an all-points bulletin that had been released about Paul. He was mocked, chained, and humiliated. He was not allowed a phone call or water to drink. When he cursed at them in response, they poured kerosene on him and lit him on fire. The scars remain on his arms and back.

Paul is a bright man, and he wrote his story. Chapter after chapter, in great detail, he wrote it all down in a spiral notebook. When Mary was on a family visit, Paul asked her if she would read it. She sat in her hotel room and finished it that evening.

When she returned his notebook, she asked Paul what he would like her to do for him, perhaps give him feedback or help with getting it published. He said, "All I'd like you to do is to write at the end of the book, 'I understand.' "[3]

We all need to be understood. That is why the gift of listening is a gift of love.

The opportunity to get it out. I came across a quote from rock musician Marilyn Manson in the documentary *Bowling for Columbine* about the murders that took place at that Colorado high school. He was asked, "If you were to talk directly to the kids at Columbine . . . what would you say to them if they were here right now?" He answered, "I wouldn't say a single word to them. I would listen to what they have to say, and that's what no one did."[4]

For those in pain, the chance to express how they feel to a trusted and valued friend is a blessing. To get their feelings out to someone who gets it. The reason this is important is basic, but it is rarely expressed.

Any time an event happens to me that has a *feeling* component, I am infused with emotional input. It leaves me in a state of imbalance, of disequilibrium. How I right the ship, how I get back in balance from the painful *input* is with *output*. I need to get my feelings out. I need to express them to someone I trust and who cares about me. *I balance the hurtful input with emotional output.*

There have been many times, perhaps in conversations with friends, that you have listened. They may be struggling, and you want to know about it. You join them in it. Perhaps there is a dilemma that they are trying to work through, and it is bothering them. They talk. And you listen. Later, in concluding, they may say, "Thank you, my friend. You have been so helpful." So helpful? But you had hardly spoken. Helpful? Yes. In your silence, you let them know that you heard them and understood. It gave them the opportunity to talk it out and, likely, to work it through.

> *I returned a phone call on my way to the kennel to pick up our dog. I did not know the man. He had been given my name as someone who might be able to offer him some direction and guidance. He was a*

manager at a local company and had an employee whom he feared could be suicidal.

A couple of minutes into our conversation and the recommendation I would give him was clear.

As he continued to talk about the crisis his colleague was going through, and how he felt in witnessing the pain, I asked for more of what it was like for him. He spoke of the fear and the helplessness. And I listened. I had long since arrived at the kennel, but our sweet terrier Holly wouldn't mind waiting a few more minutes. He talked, and I listened.

Oh, yes, I did give him my recommendation. Likely it was what he was going to do anyway.

I'm glad he called. There was much he needed to say.

The Art of Listening

We need to listen. We want to hear those who need to be heard. So, what are the keys to remember in this art of listening?

Care. Authentically care.

If you care, they will know it. If you care, they will feel it. They will feel connected, valued, and buoyed by your heartfelt support. But the compassion has to be real and from the heart.

All of us who write about the art of listening eventually mention those communication skills that facilitate others knowing they are being heard. Eye contact, focused attention, follow-up questions asked at the right time . . . all are hallmarks of effective listening.

These are important for us to have in our awareness as we sit in the presence of someone who needs to be heard. Yet this important list becomes so unimportant when we truly care.

You see, when we authentically care, our eyes automatically are focused on the person and our attention equally riveted on his or her story. Out of our compassion our questions for clarity and our expressions of concern flow naturally.

I know some fine people who have never heard of a communication technique. They never will, and they will never need to, because they care. And those for whom they care see it in their eyes, hear it in their voices, and feel it from their hearts.

Focus on them.

This moment isn't about us. As we listen we intentionally shift the focus away from ourselves. We temporarily set aside our needs, our thoughts, and our concerns in order to be with hurting ones in theirs. We listen. We want to hear their story, about the moment, the event that caused this heartache. We want to give them the opportunity to tell us about it. Our focus is on them because we care and want them to know they are not alone.

Pay attention.

As purely as we can, we give them our undivided attention.

We live in a world where there is something electronic on all the time. Usually it involves a screen. Compassionate listening requires us to break away from all the distractions. This is not a time to multitask. The hurting person deserves *all* of our attention.

Then we have to overcome the internal chatter. It's a struggle to listen to *you* when all I can hear is *me*—about the calls I need to make, the stop at the drugstore, the emails to return, the gift to buy. If we are to listen meaningfully, we must shut off the conversation in our own heads and pay attention only to the conversation with them.

When your mind strays—and it will—bring it back to the person to whom you are listening. Silently whisper "focus" to yourself. Give him or her your full attention. Auditory neuroscientist Seth Horowitz writes, "The difference between the sense of hearing and the skill of listening is attention."[5]

Our willingness to listen quietly tells them they are valued, their story is worth hearing, and we are genuinely interested in their lives.

Be sure they are feeling heard.

When someone from whom you have earned trust and respect brings a struggle to you, there are essentially three ways of responding:

- listening
- asking questions
- giving feedback

And that is the order of importance to most people. Listening, hearing them out, letting them express it to one who cares is, by far, the most important. As they are supported, their perspective is validated and their feelings confirmed. Author E. E. Cummings put it this way, "We do not believe in ourselves until someone reveals that something deep inside us is valuable, worth listening to, worthy of our trust, sacred to our touch."[6]

Asking questions about what they are saying is an important part of listening. You are inviting them to expand, to tell more, and likely to open up at a deeper level. Your questions are open-ended. Your intention is to get to know more about where they are at this important moment. But an inevitable result of your asking is they feel heard and affirmed.

First you listen, fully listen. You ask in order to hear more. You may later have some things to say, input to share. Having listened sensitively to them, they will readily listen to you. But giving feedback, when the issue of the moment is of the heart, is the least important. The feedback that matters is the message of support and caring.

To be a friend, spouse, or parent means refining the art of listening. Above all else, love them in a way that they know they are heard—that makes a connection with them that nothing else will. Our willingness to listen quietly tells them they are valued, their story is worth hearing, and we are genuinely interested in their lives.

Give them time to open up.

Patient listening gives them the time and the comfortable space to get around to those most important issues and feelings. Often they will discover in the conversation with you ways they are feeling they hadn't even realized. Those often painful, often crucial issues emerge slowly and only after there is enough room for it—uncluttered by words and agendas imposed on them. These issues are invited, not rushed.

Psychologist James Hillman writes, "For the other person to open and talk requires a withdrawal of the [listener]. I must withdraw to make room for the other . . . . This withdrawal, rather than going-out-to-meet the other, is an intense act of concentration . . . withdrawal of myself aids the other to come into being."[7]

By "withdrawal" Hillman means being quiet, while being engaged and connected. It is not withdrawal as in backing away. *It is a leaning-in listening.* It's intentional. Though it is a quiet experience, it is most active.

Then, when we speak, the focus is still clearly on them and their needs.

Unlike social conversation where we are often thinking about what we are going to *say* next, here it is more often what we are going to *ask* next.

I'm afraid there is much truth to Stephen Covey's words, "Most people do not listen with the intent to understand; they listen with the intent to reply. They are either speaking or preparing to speak."[8] We listen with the intent to hear and to understand. We give them time and room, unhurried.

Don't interrupt.

In Atul Gawande's book *Being Mortal*, he describes accompanying his father to a visit with his physician, Dr. Edward Benzel, at the Cleveland Clinic. "Benzel had a way of looking at people that let them know he was really looking at them. He was several inches taller than my parents, but he made sure to sit at eye level. . . . He did not twitch or fidget or even react when my father talked. He had that midwesterner's habit of waiting a beat after people have spoken before speaking himself, in order to see if they are really done."[9]

To interrupt or to jump in too quickly—even if it is out of eagerness to join them—may communicate that what we have to say is more important than what they are saying. They may quietly retreat.

Waiting that single beat communicates there is no rush here. Take your time. The stage is *theirs*, and we are here for *them*.

Encourage their stories.

If what they bring is a hurt, especially their grief from a death, encourage their stories. "Tell me about your dad. What was he like?" They will tell you about the time that . . . and all the ways that he would . . . and the stories may go on and on. You listen. Then you ask for more. And in the telling, something happens. In the tears and in the laughter of remembering the relationship out loud, healing happens.

I stumbled onto the importance of the telling of stories. Prior to doing my clinical training as a pastoral counselor, I was a parish minister for several years. Occasionally, a member of my church would ask me if I would conduct a funeral service for a family member, perhaps for a father who had just died and did not have a church home. Of course I would.

It became my routine to ask them to gather all the immediate family members together the next evening, bringing their memories and their stories of their dad. My motivation began solely for my sake, so they could acquaint me with this man whom I had never met. I asked them to bring their most descriptive adjectives and their *favorite* stories of him. I wanted the service to be personal to him, so I needed to know him and share some of the stories that defined his life.

On that evening we would gather. Usually it was his wife, the adult children, and their spouses. They would begin telling me their stories about this fine man. One story would be tender. Another hilarious. Another slightly off-color. Yet another downright embarrassing. Sometimes they cried. With the next story they laughed and cried some more. Emotions of every type flowed. It was beautiful. Two hours later I had all the memories and stories I needed to honor this man's life at the service the next day.

A pattern developed. I would get notes of thanks in the following weeks. There would be the gracious "atta boy" about the service, but the heart of the note was clearly one of gratitude for the evening before. They were thanking me for getting the family together, thanking me for inviting them to tell their stories.

My initial purpose in the invitation to gather that evening was for me—to get to know their dad so his service could be personal to him. What happened in that gathering was so much more important.

As they told their stories, each became a picture for their album of memories of their husband and dad that they would take with them and cherish for the rest of their lives.

Get them to tell their stories.

Listen for the score as you hear the lyrics.

In the field of psychology there is the classic phrase of "listening with the third ear."

Again, we turn to the wisdom of Hillman as he parallels this to meditation and prayer, listening for the still, small voice.

Listening for the meaning behind the message, for what is being felt behind what is being said.

"Did you know there was an immediate lilt to your voice as you spoke of . . ." you may well begin your thought, sharing an instinct you feel about what she just expressed—and suddenly a light bulb comes on within her, illuminating a new awareness you facilitated.

Third-ear listening is to hear the *feeling* behind the words, to listen for the musical score with which the lyrics are sung. You may say something like, "It sounds like that moment was especially important to you. Would you tell me more?" and your friend launches into describing a pivotal time, the significance of which he had never realized.

Ask for clarity and confirmation.

"What I hear you saying is that . . ." is the classic opening to this question. It's called mirroring, when we mirror back what we have heard for confirmation or correction. I know it sounds like a technique, and I regret that, since techniques always feel sterile and impersonal. Yet even if a technique, it's one that is warm and caring.

When I listen attentively and then ask, "If this is what you said," I have just told you that I am listening carefully and want to make sure I hear you accurately. Your words, and the feelings from which they come, matter to me.

And I want to make sure I get them right.

Remember when *you* were at a similar point in your life.

Identify with where they are, as best you can. Put yourself in their frame of reference. When were you in a similar place?

Remember? Remember what you needed and didn't need when you were there?

You probably needed, above all else, to know that you were not alone—for someone patiently to be with you and listen to you. What you likely did *not* need was for someone to get in your way. You did not need someone to interrupt you as you plowed through the emotional work before you.

We care enough to ask. And then we listen.

To talk and talk and talk with someone who cares and wants to listen may be the most healing experience one can have.

Remember. Remember when you were there. It is the single best reminder to be silent and listen.

Never Assume. Always Ask.

Never assume—never, ever assume—that you know how they feel. Ask, and then be quiet.

There are several dangers in assuming we know how they feel. The first is, even if we are right, we cheat them out of the experience of sharing it with us and the catharsis of getting their feelings out. And we cheat both of us out of that personal moment in the relationship as we hear and understand.

But, more importantly, often our hunches are not right! There are simply too many possibilities as to how they may be feeling at this moment, and if we make assumptions, then we are projecting the way we would feel onto them.

So we remember *never to assume* our resonance is identical with what they are feeling.

What we feel may be deeply experienced, but it is *our* empathetic resonance—*not theirs*. It is what their pain is triggering *in us*. It may well be the emotions we would feel were we in their shoes, but that may not be emotionally where *they* are.

So we ask. We care enough to ask. *And then we listen.*

"Please tell me about it."
"What has that been like for you?"
"How are you doing with it?"

We ask. Open-ended questions. We ask because we want to know. And we ask as an invitation for them to share.

Out of compassion we invite them to talk. It is such a simple thing. An invitation to open up and speak from the heart. But to those who suffer and have carried the burden alone, our simple invitation may be nothing short of a gift from God.

The sacred is known in relationships—in Christ's spirit of compassion and grace.

The sacred happens when one person has the courage to be open, to be personal, to share from the soul. And the other person has the grace, intentionally and attentively, to be quiet. This is the sacred silence we call *listening*.

CHAPTER 5

The Spirit of Compassion

Clothe yourselves with compassion, kindness, humility,
meekness, and patience.
—Colossians 3:12

The most important guidance I can give, as you offer your compassion to anyone suffering one of life's heartaches, is to *slip off your sandals.*

Always remember to slip
off your sandals.

We remember when Moses caught sight of the burning bush "and turned aside to see" (Exodus 3:4). God spoke to Moses and directed him: "Remove the sandals from your feet, for the place on which you are standing is holy ground" (v. 5).

Always remember to slip off your sandals. In the midst of their anguish, you are standing on sacred ground. This moment is as tender as it gets. Always treat it with the respect and sensitivity it deserves.

You walk into the home of friends. Their child has died. You came to care. The food is on the kitchen table. Family and a few friends have gathered. The talk is restrained and hushed. You look through the dining room and there, standing alone in the sun-room, is the mother. She is staring out the window into the back yard—at an empty play set. Her eyes are red, her face drawn. You take a deep breath and take your first step toward her. Slip off your sandals.

You ask about the father and are told he is up-stairs. There he sits in the bedroom with his head in his hands, sobbing. Uncontrollably. So much has been lost, so much to grieve. Without a word, you go to him and put your hand on his shoulder—squeezing with the firm grip of compassion. As you take those final few steps toward him, remember to slip off your sandals.

Back in the den, in the middle of the floor, sits their son playing with his cars. A toe-headed four-year-old, uncharacteristically somber, moving the cars slowly, without a sound. Looking more through them than at them—with his confused gaze on something a thou-sand miles away. He could use some company. You slip off your sandals and ease your aging body slowly to the floor.

In the living room at the far end of the sofa, sit-ting alone, is the precious child's grandmother. She is a strong woman but looks dazed. Where does she be-gin? Her daughter has just lost a child. She needs her mother like never before—as does her son-in-law up-stairs. Then the dear grandmother looks through the doorway to her grandson on the floor. Where does she begin? It's so confusing. Oh, yes . . . and she has her own grief. Her adored granddaughter has just died. Where does she begin? As you walk over to introduce yourself, remember your sandals.

Kindness is not something you do as much as someone you become.

We honor the significance of the moment as we address someone who needs our compassion. We access a deeper place in ourselves. We relate from the compassion of the heart. Sometimes that shift is intuitive. Sometimes it is intentional. It is always needed.

As we bring our best, we relate from our most personal selves. We bring a soulful orientation as we feel the compassion. We bring a certain spirit. We access a spirit of compassion in all its dimensions, for we are stepping onto sacred ground.

A Spirit of Kindness

And what does the Lord require of you
but to do justice, and to love kindness,
and to walk humbly with your God?
—Micah 6:8

Kindness is love in action. The motivation is love. The result is a life of kindness. With a beautiful simplicity in phrasing, Paul wrote, "Love is kind" (1 Corinthians 13:4).

Kindness is not something you do as much as someone you become. It's a way of living in the world, a way of relating wherever you are, with whoever you are. Kindness is to relate out of a spirit of grace.

"Kindness" is linguistically related to the word *kin*. Kin refers to the natural feeling we all have for the welfare of our families. Then there are "kindred spirits" with whom we feel a special affinity or kinship.

But kindness, as in loving-kindness, expands the focus beyond family or kindred spirits. It points to our wish for the best and our willingness to do what we can for the sake of anyone in the family of humankind. *Kindness* belongs with *kin* and *kinship*, for we are all related. Remember how Jesus put it, "Just as you did it to one of the least of these *who are members of my family*, you did it to me" (Matthew 25:40, italics mine).

Kindness involves sensitivity and thoughtfulness. Kindness can encourage and connect. It can transform. It is to get outside my self-interest and focus my attention on you and our connecting in this moment.

A simple moment of kindness reminds us we are all in this together. We are all kin. Kindness is consistently tender. It is always gracious and generous. It is to be caring and respectful. As Ian MacLaren said, "Be kind, for everyone you meet is fighting a great battle."

> *I was waiting as patiently as possible to mail my package. I was standing in one of those long lines at the post office. Finally, I was next. Yet the wait continued. And continued. The woman ahead of me—how shall I put this?—was being difficult. She was not blatantly hostile. Just difficult, pushy, and obsessively questioning every detail. She could not have found a kinder, more accommodating gentleman anywhere in the*

postal system. He calmly, thoroughly answered her every question with no hint of irritation or impatience.

She, at long last, finished, and I stepped up to the counter. "You were remarkably courteous to the lady ahead of me," I said to him. I shall always remember his response. As he took my package, he said simply, "You just never know what folks are going through."

Kindness has a gentle spirit. It's a tough world out there. The challenges, the battles are real. The world is filled with those who deserve a word spoken with kindness.

A simple moment of kindness reminds us we are all in this together.

I am married to someone who embodies kindness and graciousness as instinctively and intentionally as anyone I have ever known. Karen and I were at her favorite grocery store the other day, and she was introducing me to her friends in the checkout line. The clerks and the baggers love to have her come through. They share with her their life stories.

As we left I was reminded of novelist George Saunders who once said in a commencement address, "Who, in your life, do you remember most fondly, with the most undeniable feelings of warmth? Those who were kindest to you, I bet."[1] That's Karen.

She smiles and speaks to people on the sidewalk with a warmth they know is genuine. What is interesting, as I walk beside her, is to see the response from total strangers. There is an initial surprise. Then a returning smile showing their appreciation at her kindness. A gracious connection is made. Their smiles continue as we walk past.

In a city of millions, she breaks through!

All it takes to touch a lonely or struggling heart is a little kindness. A simple moment of kindness reminds us we are all in this together. We are all kin. We are family. Kindness can transform, can encourage, can connect us all.

A Spirit of Presence

You bestow on him blessings forever;
you make him glad with the joy of your presence.
—*Psalm 21:6*

Presence is to give full attention.

We are here, and nowhere else. We know the importance of the moment. We want to be here. Nothing else matters as we sit together. We don't work to keep the conversation going. We are connected. We talk. We sit in silence. Together.

Remember when you lost someone you dearly loved? Remember the moments you most valued? Remember what meant the most to you at the reception following the memorial service? It wasn't fancy words. In fact, you likely don't remember a single word anyone spoke. What meant the world to you were *the faces and the embraces*.

What meant the world was the compassion of those who came to be with you. When you spoke to them you saw in their eyes they came for no other reason than to be there for you. They spoke, of course, but they didn't have to speak. You saw it in their eyes and felt it in their hearts as they offered you the blessing of their presence and the gift of a soulful resonance.

The connection begins with an intentional presence. I value the way psychiatrist Daniel Siegel thinks about the importance of presence. Presence, he says, is necessary for *attunement*, the taking in of the heart of our friend's experience. In turn, attunement leads to *resonance*, in which two individuals engage in a personal, compassionate time together.[2] Out of that resonance one feels truly heard, understood, and no longer alone.

Deep compassion requires that we are fully present, fully attentive. It means we are in the moment. Presence involves setting aside anything that may distract us from focusing on the relationship before us. When we are completely present, the other's needs are given the respect and sensitivity he or she deserves. When our minds wander, we bring the person back to the moment. Because our friend matters. Because we care. "For where two or three are gathered in my name, I am there among them," Jesus said (Matthew 18:20). When we are truly present—heart, soul, and mind—two have just gathered.

> *A pastor friend of mine recalled one of those embarrassing moments from the early days of his ministry. He had gone to visit a parishioner who was in the hospital. The truth be told, as he made this visit, his mind was as much on writing the sermon for the coming Sunday as it was on this church member's health. It was a busy day, but he had gotten by to see her. After a rather brief visit, he said, "Well, let's have a prayer together, and I'll be on my way."*
>
> *She responded, "You might as well leave. You've had your bags packed ever since you got here."*

Ouch! That hurt. But, she was right.

We've all been there—those times we may have been in the geographical proximity but were hardly *present*. Most of us tend to live in the past or in the future, by which we are cheated of the present moment. Our relationships are cheated as well. And we all struggle with getting outside ourselves, and our own needs and interests, to be truly available to others. Being self-focused isn't a bad thing—it's an extension of our God-given survival instinct—but it has to be set aside for a time if we are truly to be present. Dr. Paul Kalanithi, in his book *When Breath Becomes Air*, describes the beginning of his journey to truly connect with his patients, "I was not yet *with* patients in their pivotal moments, I was merely *at* those pivotal moments."[3]

True connection is always a slowly developing process. It can be nurtured, facilitated, and developed, but it cannot be hurried.

I have periodically volunteered at Hospice Atlanta. I'm not there professionally as a pastoral counselor or a chaplain. I simply volunteer, to read to the patients. Some want me to read Scripture, but most of the men like sports and the women prefer poetry. After several of Mary Oliver's poems we often will chat for a moment. And then sit in silence. There are no words for the transition before them. If there is anything of value I bring, I hope it is *presence*—knowing they are not alone.

And isn't that need just as true for us all?

Priest and writer Henri Nouwen put it this way, "The friend

who can be silent with us in a moment of despair or confusion, who can stay with us in an hour of grief and bereavement, who can tolerate not knowing, not curing, not healing, and face with us the reality of our powerlessness, that is the friend who cares."[4]

> *Psychiatrist Robert Coles was doing research on children suffering the stress of poverty in the mid-sixties. He accompanied Senator Robert Kennedy on a fact-finding tour of the Mississippi delta.*
>
> *Senator Kennedy was talking with one man, a father, who was an extreme victim of the poverty of the region. "What do you say," the Senator asked, "when your girl here wants more to eat and it isn't there?"*
>
> *He responded simply, "That there isn't more now." And then he added, "I try to be calm when I speak, and sometimes I'll say tomorrow will be coming soon, and with it some food, and sometimes I'll hold the little one tight, and she'll feed off that, you know—the closeness."[5]*

The closeness. This father's phrase touches my heart. The closeness. We do feed off that. And it nourishes and nurtures us in ways words cannot describe.

A Spirit of Patience

Love is patient.
>   —*1 Corinthians 13:4*

Healing happens only with time and nurture.

> *As I understand the geography, had Moses led the people of Israel northeast after crossing the Red Sea,*

*they could have made it to their ultimate destination
of Canaan within a matter of weeks.*

*Instead he crossed the sea and turned right, going
south to Sinai.*

Why the delay?

His people weren't ready *for the Promised Land.
The healing of old wounds and claiming new attitudes*
takes time. *It can't be hurried. Growth, understanding, and spiritual maturity had to come first.*

*If Moses had stayed on his original course, they
could have easily arrived at Canaan within weeks.
But without the healing, growth, and spiritual maturity, it wouldn't have been the Promised Land.*

Similarly, our own healing, growth, and maturity take time—
it is a process. We can *facilitate* healing, we can *set the stage* for
healing—but we can't rush it any more than we can hurry a rose
to bloom.

"To suffer, to endure, and to be patient" is the meaning of
the Latin *pati*, the root word of compassion.[6] Endurance and
patience are at the heart of any compassionate relationship. For
major wounds to heal, issues to be resolved, or relationships to
be reconciled takes time.

You don't get to the Promised Land (of health, understanding, trust) without unhurried patience. Our friend who is suffering needs to be patient with her own healing process, and I need
to be equally patient as I sit with her, listen to her pain, and help
her work it through. We shift into a lower, more patient, calmer
gear.

As we endure what may feel like a marathon together, our
relationship grows. Trust, credibility, confidence of our caring
comes from unrushed support. Relationships deepen only with

time and attention—true connection is always a slowly developing process. It can be nurtured, facilitated, and developed, but it cannot be hurried. It takes time. You can't rush closeness. "Love is patient," as Paul so succinctly put it.

A Spirit of Humility

And all of you must clothe yourselves with humility in your dealings with one another, for

"God opposes the proud,
but gives grace to the humble."

—1 Peter 5:5

Jesuit priest Anthony de Mello of India once said, "In your land it is regarded as a miracle if God does someone's will. In our country it is regarded as a miracle if someone does the will of God."[7]

In this spirit, we humble ourselves to a greater call, for a greater good. With that spirit, we focus our priority on the finest values of our faith, compassion, and loving-kindness. Humility keeps us grounded in who we are and in what we honor.

As we are listening to others' pain over any issue, our agenda is to connect with them where they are. *Their* story is the agenda. Our stories are always in the background. Even when we are telling ours, theirs is the reason for the telling. We tell ours better to illuminate theirs—and to let them know they are not alone on this journey.

But our focus is never diverted from their needs and their narrative.

Intentional humility is needed in moments of compassion. The word *humble* comes from the Latin *humus*, meaning "ground" or "earth." Feet firmly planted. "Down to earth," as they say. Humility impedes any inflation of ego or pride that lifts us off that grounding. It resists distractions into vanity or self-absorption. There is less need to claim the stage for ourselves, to make it about us.

With humility, we can be there for them.

Saint Catherine of Siena expressed it in a way that translates across the centuries, "No virtue . . . can have life in itself except through charity, and humility, which is the foster-mother and nurse of charity."[8]

In the same spirit, the word *ministry* comes from the Latin *minor*, which literally translates "lesser." Anyone who is engaged in ministry, ordained or not, is one who serves another. Ministry, in all its arenas, is a humble form of service.

Confusion sometimes emerges in understanding the concepts of humility and low self-esteem. There is no similarity between the two. As someone once said, "Humility isn't thinking less of yourself, but thinking of yourself less."

Not only is there no correlation between humility and low self-esteem, those who are genuinely humble are solidly grounded in who they are. They can affirm who they are—the gifts they bring without pride or grandiosity and the weaknesses they have without shame. As the Scriptures of the Apocrypha put it, "Honor yourself with humility, / and give yourself the esteem you deserve" (Sirach 10:28).

There are times I hear the phrase about someone being "the smartest person in the room." And there are times we are all in rooms and have the feeling that is just what some people are trying to show. But humility shifts the focus away from self-aggrandizement to relationship and connection, or to the creative process of the group.

I have a friend who often is the smartest one there. Yet, out of a notably gracious spirit, she sits back as the rest hold forth. When there is a pause, she will turn to those who haven't spoken and warmly draw them out. She lets their lights shine. It's done so effortlessly you don't realize in the moment that not only did she shun the spotlight for herself, she turned it to shine on us all.

As Peter encouraged in his epistle, "Clothe yourselves with humility in your dealings with one another" (1 Peter 5:5).

Anything resembling self-centeredness blocks true compassion.

Now, anyone can do good deeds, but if the motivation is for self-centered purposes or to look compassionate in others' eyes or to earn an egotistical merit badge . . . well, it won't pass the litmus test of compassion. Humility is about submitting to a cause greater than ourselves.

It was one of those beautiful, small moments we knew we would take with us. In early May, it was Senior Recognition Sunday at our church. All high school graduating seniors stood before the congregation to be recognized. They stepped to the microphone and each, in turn, gave us their name, their high school, and the college they would be attending the coming fall. A shout of "Go Dawgs" or "Roll Tide" would often follow.

On this Sunday, the front pews were reserved for the seniors. After their recognition, they each returned to their places and were seated. Slowly the pews refilled. Only something had happened. Perhaps a student or two had returned to the wrong row, and the last pew was filling up too quickly. The rows were full, and there wouldn't be enough room for them all.

The last senior to speak was reserved and timid, a little shy. She had not been active in the youth group and likely didn't feel that she quite belonged. I had the sense she wanted no extra attention drawn to her— and I was helplessly watching it play out as she was about to be the one without a place to sit. She approached her pew as the girl before her, Jessie, was about to take the last spot.

I watched as Jessie paused before sitting. She looked back and realized what was about to happen. Then with remarkable grace, Jesse stepped back into the aisle and gestured for the other girl to take the remaining seat. We then watched as Jessie, with a beautiful humility, took her place in the aisle, on the floor.

A friend in advertising tells me that everyone listens to one radio station: WII-FM—*What's in It for Me.* The attitude of compassion is, *What's in it for you?* The person who is humble knows who he is, feels solid about it, and has no need for the moment to be about him. "Learn from me," Jesus said, "for I am gentle and humble in heart, and you will find rest for your souls" (Matthew 11:29). With a spirit of gentle humility, the ones who need our care feel our attention. It is a safe, restful place for their souls.

I am reminded of that tense scene from the Scriptures, when a heated discussion broke out over the future seating arrangements on the dais in the kingdom of heaven. The other disciples were unhappy after the request had been made that perhaps James and John could be seated at Jesus's right and at his left. Can't you just see Jesus's expression? I picture him looking down, his head slowly shaking. How badly they didn't get it. It was in that moment Jesus redefined what greatness really means. "Whoever wishes to be great among you must be your servant, and whoever wishes to be first among you must be your slave" (Matthew 20:26-27).

"You are the light of the world," is Jesus's way of reminding us of our true identity.

Jesus's kind of greatness requires humility. Humility is about submitting to a greater cause—and thus connecting us to our deepest selves.

A Spirit of Light

"You are the light of the world. . . . let your light shine before others."
                                        —*Matthew 5:14, 16*

At Children's Hospital in Atlanta a six-year-old girl was gently placed on a gurney and wheeled into the operating room to repair her broken elbow. It was not unusual. The medical staff sees these injuries all the time, from gymnastics to jungle gyms to falling off skateboards.

But this girl's broken elbow was different. Medically it was like all the others, but the cause was different. There was no skateboard or bicycle involved. No, this little girl broke her elbow from falling into a Dumpster while searching for food for herself and her younger siblings.

After hearing of this child's accident, I happened to be scheduled to read to our middle grandson's kin-

dergarten class. Reading to fifteen five- and six-year-olds—well, it was a trip. I looked at them with those sparkling eyes and beautiful smiles. I savored the time with them and their fascination with the stories. Then I remembered the little girl at Children's, searching for food in a Dumpster. She was exactly the same age.

We remember our Lord's metaphor and inspiration for our loving-kindness. "You are the light of the world . . . let your light shine before others." As we offer ourselves, our intent is to *be the light*. It's more than being good. It's about being the *light*.

And what exactly is "being the light?" Here Paul is again helpful. The light, as Paul phrased it, is "the Christ in you." The soulful grace, the compassion, the caring, the loving-kindness—that is the light.

This is what Jesus was talking about when he said, "You are the light of the world." You are *his* light for the world. And that light and its compassion, combined with the grace of God, may touch hearts and give those we meet the inspiration to better deal with the challenges in their lives.

At our core is the image and likeness of God (Genesis 1:26). This essential grace can become so buried beneath layers of superficial attitudes and self-images that we lose sight of the sacred implanted within each of us. I love the way Father Richard Rohr emphasizes that "Our core is original blessing, not original sin."[9]

We are to be the light in any context, in any direction to which we feel called. Often it will be in relationships with those we know and even love. Or perhaps it will come out of an awareness of a struggle with someone outside our social realm, or even a stranger we encounter into whose darkness we can bring a moment of light. For many there is a "social empathy" they feel in which this same emotion brings compassion to make a wider change. Names immediately spring to mind—Nelson Mandela, Pope Francis, Mohandas Gandhi, Martin Luther King Jr.—of those who saw a social darkness and gave their lives to being the light.

"You are the light of the world," is Jesus's way of reminding us of our true identity. Then, "Let your light shine" is his call to live out that identity, to be who—in our heart of hearts—we truly are.

The little girl at Children's Hospital was gently placed on a gurney and wheeled into the operating room to repair her broken elbow—from landing at the bottom of a Dumpster.

We feel a call to do our part, to make the world a little more beautiful, a little more loving, a little brighter . . . for her. You are the light of the world.

PART II

Compassion of the Soul

CHAPTER 6

The Gift of Grace

From his fullness we have all received, grace upon grace.
—John 1:16

The grace of God is what fuels this whole compassionate adventure. *The experience of grace invites us to the dance.* To know in the depth of our souls the mystery that we are loved, we are accepted, we are embraced by the grace of the God of our creation—this is what sends us off to share something of that same grace.

"We love because he first loved us," as John wrote (1 John 4:19). In order to give, we first receive.

Listen to the voices of those who truly care. As you hear their words, listen for the tone, the inflection of how they speak. Whether they express themselves softly or passionately, you hear it. There is a certain quality. There is a heartfelt caring. It comes from a place of *grace*. It is at the heart of what makes them who they are. From their experience of grace come those qualities of compassion, empathy, and loving-kindness.

In a phrase, *they care*. Others matter. They care with compassion. They are coming from a deeper place than most. When they are with you, you know you matter to them. You are not being used or manipulated or simply enjoyed. You are valued. With them, you are in relationship.

Grace might well be defined as "God's love spoken with a softer voice."

This entire writing is a call to care. But please know that to care is not simply a decision. At its deepest and finest, caring comes from who we are, from who we have become. It began with receiving love and acceptance. Our compassion, then, is a response to that grace.

Grace transforms us into something more than we were before.

When we have spiritual moments of affirmation, of forgiveness, of reconciliation, of acceptance, moments of God's own presence, our souls are filled with an abundance we instinctively want to share.

We are changed by God's grace. We are transformed. We reach out with compassion from a more substantial place.

Grace

Grace is a word with a beauty and a richness of its own. We are drawn to it. We long for it. We feel it as much as we understand it. It speaks to the heart. We struggle to define grace. It's hard to nail down, though; as the cliché goes, we know it when we see it.

Grace is warm, tender, personal, loving, always welcomed and, well . . . gracious. And it tends to come in small packages. Think about it—when we are overwhelmed with good fortune we tend to call it a "blessing." "I felt so *blessed* with the wonderful news," we hear ourselves say. But when blessings are more personal we tend to refer to them as "moments of grace." Though it would never fit in any dictionary, perhaps grace might well be defined as *"God's love spoken with a softer voice."*

But a softly spoken word of grace can change our world and make all the difference.

It was one of those common, everyday settings in which nothing memorable was about to happen. I was about eight years old. We made a stop for snacks on a family trip. As we came out of the store, I happened to be leading our family back to the car. Walking between two cars, my way was blocked by an elderly lady trying to get into her car.

I remember my focus was on her hand as she was trying to open the door. It was absolutely frail. Remember now, these were cars of the '50s when you grasped the door handle and pressed the button to release the latch. I stood there watching her struggle, gripping the handle with her thumb pressing with all the strength she had. Nothing budged.

I didn't know what to do. So I did nothing but stare. I was a decent kid, but I honestly had no idea what to do. I wanted to help her, but I didn't want to embarrass her. I was the poster child for the deer-in-the-headlights. I stood frozen in that awkward moment for what felt like an embarrassing eternity, until over my shoulder I saw the tall figure of my dad walking past me. I heard him say to her, "You know, sometimes those handles get stuck and are so hard to open. May I try?" She smiled and stepped back,

*and my dad's big hand grabbed the handle. I think
he paused for a moment so it wouldn't look too easy,
and he opened her door. She gratefully thanked him
and got into her car.*

*"Sometimes those handles get stuck and are so hard
to open. May I try?" Compassion spoken with grace.*

*It was a simple moment I've carried with me over
all these years. A simple, sacred moment of grace.*

*From your childhood you have your own. These
are the times when compassion is shared, and you
have experienced a moment of grace.*

The gift of grace comes, and is delivered, in these small
packages. It may not seem remarkable, but having received,
unwrapped, and opened the small gift, *our lives are changed.*
Grace tends to slip in with no announcement, no fanfare.

And in that moment, it *transforms our world*—like a child
being born in a stable and gently placed in a manger.

Gran, pretend we're dancing. Grace. Grace can turn moments of awkwardness into moments of joy. Grace becomes the
dance. Grace can transform the ordinary into something sacred.
We hear it, and we feel its warmth. The word has several different uses:

He played the piece with effortless *grace.*

She had all the social *graces.*

He fell from *grace.*

He was given another month's *grace.*

She *graced* us with her presence.

We were in her good *graces.*

Before we ate, he said *grace.*

And, of course, "Amazing *Grace.*"[1]

Every use of this versatile word, whether it refers to

> elegance,
>> courtesy,
>>> deferment,
>>>> gift, or
>>>>> blessing

is positive and nurturing. We feel it as much as understand it. It speaks to the heart as well as the mind.

Christian writer Frederick Buechner wrote of grace, "After centuries of handling and mishandling, most religious words have become so shopworn nobody's much interested any more. Not so with *grace*, for some reason. Mysteriously, even derivatives like *gracious* and *graceful* still have some of the bloom left."[2] Author Philip Yancey points to the same truth when he referred to grace as "'the last best word' because every English usage I can find retains some of the glory of the original."[3]

So grace is a process. It is first something we receive, then something we become.

The Latin origin, *gratia*, means "something that merits gratitude, a service rendered."[4] Gratia's offspring also include gratitude, gratuity, gratify, and even congratulations. There is a love and goodness about the word—and the linguistic company it keeps—pointing to the holy. The Greek for grace, *charis*, is the origin of "eucharist." Grace implies a gift, one that is freely shared and offered with generosity.

The understanding of grace evolved into two distinct, yet related, meanings. The first is "the free and unmerited favor of God,"[5] and the second, "a virtue coming from God."[6] The first is a blessing we receive from God. The latter is the result, a quality of character within us inspired by God. The two are consistently connected. Grace is a process. It is in motion. Ultimately, grace is transformational.

Grace is first an experience of being graced, an awareness of the gift, and then the resulting transformation. We receive it. We are touched by it. We are changed. Grace then becomes something we *are*.

This is where compassion comes in. The experience of the transformation evokes a response. As Rabbi Alvin Sugarman put it so beautifully, "Our lives should be a thank-you note to God."[7] Out of our gratitude, grace becomes something we want to offer—to live with grace, to be compassionate, to be loving, to be gracious.

Again, "We love because he first loved us."

> *Because we first are loved, we seek to be more loving.*
> *Because we first are blessed, we want to be a blessing.*
>> *Because we first are served, we seek to be of service.*
>>> *Because we first receive grace, we want to be more gracious.*

So grace is a process. It is first something we receive, then something we become. It is first a blessing, then transformed into a virtue. Grace comes from beyond us. It is experienced. Then, if we allow ourselves to be changed by it, grace takes on a human face.

Without the inspiration of grace, our acts of compassion are simply good deeds. They are well intended and thankfully received but likely not sustainable. Without the soul and the heart, our deeds will lack the motivation that empowers our compassion and fortifies its depth and meaning.

Compassion begins with grace, for there is its source and inspiration.

First, we must be open to receiving the grace.

The Awareness of Grace

Life itself—to awaken this morning—is grace.

One summer, my wife, Karen, and I spent a glorious week in the Canadian Rockies. We stayed in a lodge overlooking a pristine, emerald lake surrounded on all sides by those magnificent mountains. Early on the morning of the last day of our stay, I arose before sunrise, put on my running gear, and struck out for my usual run around the lake. Don't be impressed; it's not a big lake.

Halfway through the run I turned to look back across those still, emerald waters. With the valley in the shadows of first light, the sun had begun to shine on Mount Vaux, its glacier brightly reflecting those first rays of morning. It was the kind of sight that would take your breath away. It took mine. It was an experience of awe.

Then I looked to the east where the mountain's sheer face shot up almost vertically. Still in the shadow the sun's rays were just beginning to shine over it. Then to the north a mountain with the beauty of one beginning to show the wear of the ages it had known—and beyond it the glacier of a peak called The President.

I kept turning. Every direction I looked was just as awe-inspiring as the one before. Each magnificent and each different. I basked in it. I savored it. I felt absolutely blessed with the privilege of being in that place at that moment.

Then I realized . . . this is my life! The Rockies were a metaphor for my own life. In every direction I turn—my marriage, my family, my friends, my faith, my vocation—in every direction I turn there are magnificent peaks of life experience, of loving relationships, of growing faith, of meaningful work.

There are also valleys, to be sure. In my life, as in yours, there are challenges, disappointments, heartaches, even tragedy; but they don't diminish the blessing.

Life itself is grace, as it has been said.

As the day breaks on any given morning, in every direction I turn there is grace. I didn't need the Rockies to experience grace. I needed the Rockies to remind me of the subtle, yet profound, grace that surrounds me daily. So why is that? Why do I need a reminder of something so potent and essential in my life, something that is so obvious once it is brought back into focus? Why? Because God speaks in that still, small voice. God allows God's own divine presence to be seen or not seen. Because so often grace is delivered in those small packages.

Years ago, Karen and I endured a horrible loss as our two-year-old son, Eric, died in an accident. You can imagine what a nightmare it was for us. A few weeks after his death, Karen was in the kitchen alone. It was a quiet morning. Our other son, Patrick, was playing in the den. I was at work.

She was feeling the depth of grief only a mother could know. She was quietly praying, "God, please help me. Please help me make it through this." Just then the phone rang. It was a dear friend of hers. She asked with a hint of urgency, "Karen, are you all right?" Karen answered, "I am now."

Grace.

Someone once said, "We can do no great things; we can do small ones with great love." That's grace. It's experienced in the smallest ways but with the transforming power of great love.

In my years as a pastoral counselor I have sat with those nearing their own deaths. In those moments, the distinction between the trivial and the substantial has never been clearer. They almost never speak of wealth or accomplishments or status. They may mention regrets or some good deeds they left undone. But, almost always, when they speak of what has touched them most deeply, they talk of family and friends. A smile comes, their voices soften, and they tell of those with whom they have shared and received love. They tell their stories about "the little things in life" with those who cared and events that transformed the moments they had together into something amazing.

"Enjoy the little things in life," someone once said, "because one day you will look back and realize they were the big things."

Grace as Something We Receive

Grace is first a gift. Theologically it is "the free and unmerited favor of God."

God's grace is a central biblical theme. As Paul put it, "For by grace you have been saved through faith, and this is not your own doing; it is the gift of God—not the results of works" (Ephesians 2:8-9). Grace always begins with God. Grace is always relational. Grace is always a gift. And grace is *always* amazing.

The grace that inspires us to compassion is the grace of relationship.

In the life of Jesus Christ, we have the clearest glimpse into the heart of God we will ever know. It was into loving relationship that he invited us and offered his grace. Relationship. Faithful, loving connection is the theme to which the Scriptures consistently invite us. The grace of God and the grace of God through others transform us and intuitively make us want to live more graciously.

Grace begins with God. We didn't earn it. We couldn't earn it. It is a free and unmerited favor.

The word *unmerited* makes many of us a little uneasy. Out of the work-ethic mentality with which most of us were reared, we hear in it the implication that we should have earned it. We should have merited it—but though we are a bunch of slackers, God is going to give it to us anyway.

But that is not the way God reasons or the way God loves. God welcomes us into relationship before we can merit it, and God welcomes us back into relationship when we haven't merited it. *Unmerited* simply emphasizes that grace is a gift, not a reward or a payment for anything we deserved or had coming. God's grace has no hint of a quid pro quo.

Grace is a gift.

Remember the times someone did something unexpected and generous for you? Out of your sincere gratitude you said, "Oh, let me reimburse you for that." To which they said, "Heavens, no. Then it wouldn't be a gift." That is precisely Paul's point as he wrote about grace, "But if it is by grace, it is no longer on the basis of works, otherwise grace would no longer be grace" (Romans 11:6).

God is at work within each of us, always inviting us into moments of grace. We are blessed just by showing up. We are blessed just by waking up to the gift of a new day. We are blessed with the awareness that within this new day will be offerings of grace. They come as gifts. When I greet a certain friend with, "Phil, how are you doing?" I consistently hear his response, "Better than I deserve." I think to myself, *I would hate to be stuck with what I deserve.*

And only because of grace, thank God, I'm not.

CHAPTER 7

The Grace of the Still Small Voice

Be still before the LORD.
—Psalm 37:7

Experiencing the grace of God may happen anywhere.

Randomly.
    Unexpectedly.
        Meaningfully.
            Delightfully.
                Anytime.
                    Anywhere.

Any form of sacred silence begins with stillness. It begins in the quiet.

A thoughtful note. A kind gesture. Countless times we have felt that grace from someone whose path we were blessed to cross. Or from a dear friend whose life has intertwined with ours for years. These are the times God's grace has a human face and is spoken with a familiar accent.

Yet there are other times I seek God's grace spiritually, intentionally, to be in God's own presence. I find these in moments of sacred silence. You may well know what I mean. These are the times we slow down our lives, quiet our minds, and move toward a place of spiritual solitude. We remember the warning that was once given—centuries ago—"Beware the barrenness of a busy life."

So we slow the pace, with time for silence. We become open to the presence of God, where we may feel God's nearness. In remarkable moments of insight, revelation, and absolute blessing . . . we may become aware of God's own voice.

The psalmist writes, "Be still, and know that I am God!" (Psalm 46:10). The very passage that invites us into a relationship with God begins with "Be still." Any form of sacred silence begins with stillness. It begins in the quiet.

In the stillness, we connect with our souls; we go to deeper places.

> In the stillness, we experience God as in no other way.
>> In the stillness, we are in touch with our true selves, the lives for which we are created and to which we are called.
>>> Out of the stillness, out of the quiet we experience peace . . . and may even know the softly spoken voice of God.

The Scriptures tell us the Lord passed by the mountain. And the wind blew, but God was not in the wind. And the earthquake shook, but God was not in the earthquake. And there was fire, but God was not in the fire. Then after all of this, *there* . . . was the presence of God . . . *in "a still small voice"* (1 Kings 19:11-12 KJV, italics mine).

A still small voice is one that can *only be heard* in the quiet, in the silence. Silence invites us to those deep places . . . within our hearts and souls.

The Struggle for Quiet

To be quiet is to turn the volume of the world all the way down.
    To be silent is to turn it completely off.
        Let's start with quiet.

My goodness, how we struggle with this, with being still and being quiet.

"Never disturb the silence, unless you can improve upon it."

We live in a world that is focused on anything but solitude. The attention that is given to screens of all sizes is remarkable. Our culture is devoted to texting, emailing, posting, or anything that prohibits the quieting of the mind, allowing the space for silence.

Ours is a time that is rushed and crowded and distracted. It's like the little sign that reads, "I'm so busy I don't know if I found a rope or lost a horse."

Then there is the clutter and chatter of all the thoughts that are constantly going through our minds. I don't know about you, but quieting this chatter is a huge challenge. *There is* always *something going on up there*. Thoughts, ideas, questions—more thoughts, more ideas, more questions. Some of it is good stuff. Most of it is *so mundane*. There are all the things I've got to remember to do: calls to make, emails to return, something to pick up, clothes to drop off at the cleaners . . . my mind is always going. Singer and songwriter Leonard Cohen described that internal hubbub, saying, "my ordinary state of mind is very much like the waiting room at the DMV."[1]

We tend to choose busy over solitude. Now, make no mistake, much of our "busy" is engaged in meaningful, thoughtful ways—caring and providing for children and family, volunteering, serving, or community involvement. Good ways.

But still, we need the balance. We each need to step back, to step away from the demands and the pressures and the responsibilities that become our lives . . . to be still, to be quiet, even silent—to "be still and know."

The Need for Silence

This path of silence and solitude is often the way of peace. The quiet peace that passes all understanding. "Peace I leave with you," Jesus said (John 14:27). Through sacred silence we claim that gift. If we so choose.

There is an old saying that is attributed to the Quakers, "Never disturb the silence, unless you can improve upon it."

We need that undisturbed silence,
    calmness,
        stillness,
            quiet,
                solitude . . . and the peace that comes with it.

In any good piece of music, there is the harmony, the balance between the notes and the silence separating the notes. As Claude Debussy reportedly said, "Music is not in the notes, but the silence between them." Without the spaces, it would be no longer music. It would just be noise.

Each human life is a symphony. Each of our lives needs the notes, the activity, the engagements . . . *and* the pauses, the spaces, the times of silence between—to keep our lives in harmony, in balance. Only then is it a symphony, as Jesus said, of a life lived abundantly (John 10:10).

That harmony is lost in lives lived at a pace with so few spaces. The result is only noise. Emotionally, then, those lives are not as healthy. Spiritually, they become empty, lacking the depth, the vibrancy God intended.

Thus, the Scriptures point us back to the themes of silence and stillness. The psalmist consistently wrote of it:

"Be still, and know that I am God." (46:10)
"For God alone my soul waits in silence." (62:1)
"Be still before the LORD, and wait patiently for him." (37:7)

As the psalmist consistently wrote of being quiet and still, Jesus consistently lived it. Time after time the Synoptic Gospels tell us he would go up into the hills to pray—to be still, in the quiet. From Matthew we read, "And after he had dismissed the crowds, he went up the mountain by himself to pray. When evening came, he was there alone" (14:23).

It doesn't strike me as coincidental that, in the verses that follow, Jesus then came down the mountain, saw the disciples in trouble as they tried to navigate their boat in the storm, and—

renewed and empowered by that time of prayerful silence—he walked on the water to meet them.

Spiritually, something powerful takes place in the quiet, in the silence, in the stillness.

The Sacred in the Silence

I invite you to take a moment to rid your mind of the clutter. All the thoughts. Let go of that nagging worry. Release that anxiety. Free your mind of it all. Clear it out . . . to listen for God's word for you in *this* sacred moment.

To be silent is to open our souls to the Sacred, which is always present.

Let's pause for a time and be perfectly quiet—not for an exercise in meditation—but simply to set the tone for our thinking together.

> *In the quiet, take a deep breath. Exhale. Breathe.*
> *Slowly turn the volume of the world all the way down.*
> *For the moment, take the day's burdens off your shoulders. Let them go.*
> *Relax.*
> *For this time, forget the hurry of this day,*
> *. . . the list of things you have to get done,*
> *forget the planning for tomorrow.*
> *Forget the week ahead with its responsibilities. You will pick them up later.*
> *Set it all aside. For this moment, let it go.*

Turn the volume down ... all the way down.
Let this moment be a sacred space.
Let the clutter, all the thoughts and ideas and tasks-
to-do, fall away as you focus on this exact moment
being a sacred time.
Turn the volume down ... and let any clutter that
separates you from time with God,
> *fall away.*
For the next few moments close your eyes, breathe
deeply and be quiet.
Just.
Be.
Still.

Isn't there quite a contrast between those moments of quiet from the rest of our lives?

To meditate, is not blocking everything out so much as making a clearing *for the presence of the divine.*

To be silent is to open our souls to the Sacred, which is always present. The Spirit is always there, awaiting our awareness. It is amusing that at the beginning of many formal occasions we have an "invocation"—invoking God's presence at the event—as if God wasn't already there. What we need to do instead is to invoke our awareness of God's ever-existing presence at that event and in every moment of our lives.

Invoking our awareness is what the "sacred silence" does. When we are silent we pause and are present and are aware of the sacred in our *midst*.

Sacred silence is not focused on beliefs but relationship. "Be still, and know that I am God" (Psalm 46:10). It's not knowing *about* God; it's knowing God. Carl Jung, the psychoanalyst of the twentieth century, was asked if he believed in God. He responded that more important than *believing* in God, he *knew* him.

Beliefs are important. My convictions, my theology, my understandings of God pave the way for this process. But if we stop with beliefs, if we think that we can *believe* our way into those divine moments, we will be disappointed. The path of encountering the divine is not nearly so much theological as it is spiritual.

Only then can we have *an experience with God*.

In his poem "Great Wagon," Rumi put it so beautifully:

> Out beyond ideas of wrongdoing and rightdoing,
> there is a field. I'll meet you there.
>
> When the soul lies down in that grass,
> the world is too full to talk about.[2]

I am reminded of the dear person who came by to see Karen and me, years ago, after the loss of our son. She shook my hand, and then just held it as she gazed at the floor. After a long pause, she tearfully looked up and gently said, "I have no words." When I am silent and experience God, like both Rumi and my friend, "I have no words."

Making a Clearing

In silent prayer, what we do—and this is the best way I have heard it expressed—is to *make a clearing*. To be in this kind of prayer, to meditate, is not *blocking everything out* so much as *making a clearing* for the presence of the divine.

I think of wildlife photographers. They can't photograph any magnificent animal as long as it is in the bushes or in the brush. The animal is revealed only in the clearing. This is what centering prayer does. It creates a clearing for the presence of God, with its wisdom and truth and grace to appear and be revealed.

How is this centering prayer done? I encourage you to seek one of many excellent workshops for that, to help you learn to clear the way. Then you can, in the relative stillness, open yourself to illuminating moments.

But, first, we slow down.

We turn off every screen of every size.

We begin to make a clearing.

We repeat those words of the psalmist: "Be still, and know that I am God."

We relax.

We breathe deeply.

We seek calmness.

We calm the chatter, clear the clutter.

Though we are in prayer, this is not when we make our intercessions to God. We can't be talking and listening at the same time. We are quiet, so we can be available for moments of experience, insight, and inspiration.

This moment is not for what we want God to know but for whatever God is about to reveal to us.

Of course, the problems or issues in our lives do not go away through prayer and meditation. They have to be addressed on their own terms. What silent prayer does is to clear the more superficial and take us to a deeper, wiser, more substantial place within ourselves—allowing us then to reengage life with a new perspective, better able to deal with those problems and issues.

It begins with making a clearing. Remember the biblical phrase about Jesus having "emptied himself" (Philippians 2:7)? This is a part of what the phrase means to me. Within his humanity he made a clearing so the divine, the sacred, within him could be experienced. He emptied himself; he opened himself so "the way, and the truth, and the life" (John 14:6) could be revealed. He then turns, and to us says, "Follow me."

The Grace of Intentional Awareness

To "be still and know" does not always require meditation. Simply awareness. There are moments throughout every day where we can be aware of the sacred in our midst. As Father Richard Rohr wrote, "There is no more infallible way to seek the will of God than moment by moment to see that what this moment offers me *is* the grace of God."[3]

Every day is alive with possibility. We are on the threshold of the sacred at every turn.

In order to experience this, we have to live attentively. We have to be present in the moment. We have to watch. We have to listen. Remember: *God tends to move quietly and speak softly.*

Without our intentional awareness throughout the day of the presence of the divine, we miss the holy. When we walk without hurry through life and are intentionally aware, we recognize and honor the sacred far more often. Without the awareness in the moment or in the quiet time of reflection afterward, we miss so much.

I was driving back across Atlanta from a speaking event late one Saturday morning. I topped a hill, and before me was backed-up traffic from road work being done. I came to a stop in the far right lane.

As I sat there something caught my eye to the right of my car. A man walked toward the passenger side of the car behind me. From my side-view mirror I saw the woman sitting there reach out and hand the man a white paper bag. It was from Dunkin' Donuts.

The man took the bag, nodded—as I am sure he was thanking her for her thoughtfulness—and walked back across the vacant lot. It was only as he approached the tree that I saw a brown duffle bag, containing his belongings, at its base.

Thank goodness the traffic continued to be held up. I saw him sit beneath the tree holding the small paper bag in both hands. Not yet knowing what it contained he bowed his head, closed his eyes, and said grace. For the longest time he gave thanks. I was touched and humbled by his gratitude.

The traffic finally began moving, and I looked back one more time to memorize that moment. I knew I was witnessing a sacrament.

Life is filled with just such sacred moments if we will watch, if we will listen, if we will be present in the moment. By some, such as this one, we are blessed. By others we are called to be the blessing.

The Wisdom from the Silence

Wisdom comes from the quiet, from the silence. Spiritual awareness comes from listening for the voice of the Spirit of

God. The purpose of intentional silence—in meditation, in prayer, in reflection, in awareness of the moment—is, first, to be aware of the presence and the nearness of divine grace.

If you are hearing the voice of God, it will be a voice of grace. God's voice always is.

Then it is to listen . . .
to listen for the voice . . .
for the voice of God's wisdom and insight and direction and inspiration.

Before Helen Keller became an icon, she was a little girl. Bright and healthy and happy. She was precocious—walking and beginning to talk by her first birthday. She loved the outdoors, the sunshine, and the blue sky above the towering pines of Alabama.

But then, at the age of nineteen months, her world went dark and silent. The year was 1882, and the diagnosis of "congestion" and "the flux" may have been medically ambiguous, but the tragic result had no ambiguity.

As a result of the illness, her sight dimmed and her hearing became increasingly faint—and by her twentieth month she was blind and deaf. The emotional impact of this was traumatic. Decades later she would write of that time, writing of herself in third person: "With appalling suddenness she (herself, Helen) moved from light to darkness and became a phantom."[4]

A phantom—a ghost—one who no longer exists. Cut off. Isolated. Alone.

And afraid. Can you imagine? She must have been as terrified as she was confused. She expressed it as rage—but remember that anger is a secondary emotion and behind every anger is fear. She was a very scared little girl.

Remember Baby Jessica? She was the eighteen-month-old little girl who fell into the abandoned well in west Texas in the mid 1980s. Alone, isolated, terrified, and out of reach—that is as close as I can get to understanding what Helen's new life was like.

Helen's world was dark and silent . . . and alone. Surrounded by those who loved her, she was alone. A self-described phantom.

With great compassion and effort, her parents found Annie Sullivan and brought her to Tuscumbia, Alabama, to work with Helen. There was much Annie did for Helen, but the key in turning on the light for her was how Annie patiently held her hand and throughout the day with one finger would write into the palm of Helen's hand the words of every object they encountered or activity they engaged. Day after day, trying to build a bridge to Helen's isolation. Day after day. Letter after letter. Word after word.

One afternoon, walking past the well house, Annie put Helen's hand under the flow of the cool water. In the palm of Helen's other hand Annie wrote slowly, W-A-T-E-R. Then more rapidly. And something miraculous happened. Here are Helen's words:

"Somehow the mystery of language was revealed to me. I knew then that W-A-T-E-R meant the wonderful cool something that was flowing over my hand. . . .I left the well-house eager to learn. Everything had

a name, and each name gave birth to a new thought. As we returned to the house every object which I touched seemed to quiver with life."[5]

She reached her! It was like the fireman, deep in that well, stretching those last inches to grasp Baby Jessica's hand. Annie reached Helen, and she was back.

She was reunited! She understood language, and it became a bridge back to the world.

This is what God does for us in the movement of the Spirit. In the moments we are blind or lost or isolated, it is as if God is taking us by the hand and beginning to write

G-R-A-C-E—and we felt his grace.

H-O-P-E—and our lives were filled with possibility.

L-O-V-E—and the wonder of God's love washed over us.

From the Book of Wisdom (18:14-15) of the Jerusalem Bible are the words,

> When peaceful silence lay over all,
> and night had run the half of her swift course,
> down from the heavens, from the royal throne, leapt
>   your all-powerful Word.

"When peaceful silence lay over all."

It is from that place of "peaceful silence" we listen . . . for the voice, for "your all-powerful Word" for our lives.

But here let me add a word of caution: You may also hear other voices. They are addressed to you, and they tend to be louder. They are the negative voices of shame, of criticism, of judgment—voices that leave you somehow diminished, a lesser person. These are the damaging echoes of voices from your past.

All of those will keep you from your true and finest self. *None of those voices are God's.* You have to listen past those voices, to clear the way to the one beyond them, to the one who speaks softly.

I don't know what God's word will be for you. But I do know that if you are hearing the voice of God, it will be a voice of grace. God's voice always is.

When I am quiet, I am most aware . . . of grace. In some form or fashion you will hear: "You are loved. You are forgiven. You are accepted. And you will always belong within my grace."

A pastor friend of mine had been asked to offer the invocation at the opening of a large convention. His name is Gene. Seated with him on the dais was a young man who was invited to sing "America" a cappella. The young man had Down syndrome.

It came his turn to sing. He stepped to the microphone and began singing proudly,

> *My country 'tis of thee,*
> *sweet land of liberty,*
> *   of thee I sing.*

At this point, something happened to him that has happened to everyone who has ever dared stand before an audience. His mind went blank. He stood there, having no idea of the next line. His smiling face was now frozen and pale.

Gene spotted the young man's panic instantly. Quietly and quickly he stood and slipped up behind him. Over the young man's shoulder, Gene softly sang,

> *of thee I sing. Land where . . .*

*and the young man's face came back to life. He took
a deep breath and sang,*

> *Land where my fathers died,
> land of the pilgrims' pride,
> from every mountain side,
>   let freedom ring.*

*He continued singing as Gene eased back to his
seat.*

Any time we lose our place or lose focus or purpose, if we
will listen, the divine voice will prompt us of our song to sing.
We need to be still, to be quiet to hear it. Make that clearing of
silence, and listen for what words of wisdom are being spoken
to you. As Samuel was directed to pray, "Speak, LORD, for your
servant is listening" (1 Samuel 3:9). Such is our prayer.

I have a friend whose life's work is meeting the needs of those
living in the poorest nations of our world. She has seen the dev-
astation of poverty few of us ever will. I have heard her say,
"When something breaks your heart, it may be God speaking to
you to do something about it."

God will speak. Yet we must be present in the moment, listening for God's will for us at that place, at that point in time.
God is available to help us discern who we are at any time, in
any circumstance of our lives.

In your times of sacred silence, what will you hear?

I don't know what word will be for your hearing. It may well
be in keeping with what Saint Frances of Assisi heard. After
an adult lifetime of quiet, contemplative prayer, these are his
words:

Lord, make me an instrument of your peace;
where there is hatred, let me sow love;
where there is injury, pardon;
where there is doubt, faith;
where there is despair, hope;
where there is darkness, light;
and where there is sadness, joy.
Grant that I may not so much seek to be consoled as
    to console;
to be understood as to understand;
to be loved as to love;
for it is in giving that we receive;
it is in pardoning that we are pardoned;
And it is in dying that we are born to eternal life.[6]

CHAPTER 8

Never Beyond the Reach
of God's Grace

The light shines in the darkness, and the darkness
did not overcome it.
—John 1:5

At every turn, there is grace. Yet I must be aware in order to
experience it.

I sit here, just now, in the sunroom of our home in the
quiet of this spring morning in Atlanta. I have my lap-
top before me, typing away on these thoughts about
grace. A truck pulls up in our neighbor's driveway,
and the driver parks not far from where I am sitting. I
suspect what is coming. The quiet of this quiet morn-
ing is about to end.

Yes, he lowers the ramp on the back of his truck
and rolls out his lawnmower. He soon cranks it and
begins mowing his first lawn of the day. Is it a distrac-
tion? Yes. Is it a disturbance? Sure. But in an odd way
it feels like a blessing. I look over my shoulder, and
there he is mowing away. I feel a kind of collegiality.

*The noise becomes a companion. Here we are—a
couple of workmen engaged in our tasks. I still have
my privacy, but I'm no longer alone.*

If I allow myself to be aware, grace can be experienced at most every turn.

*PS—He is now quietly trimming the neighbor's
shrubs. Quiet company. Grace upon grace.*

Over the years I have often spoken and taught on the theme of grace. Consistently I have had to restrain my impatience. Knowing there is a world of hurt and need just beyond our doorstep, I have been tempted to rush us from the experience of grace to the desire to be gracious, to move readily from being blessed to being a blessing.

First, we must know the grace. First, we must receive the blessing.

Pause in this moment, know that you are loved, and stop there.

Know that you eternally matter to the God who created you, and stop there.

Know that you are always within the reach of God's grace, and stop there.

Let this moment be about you.

Not So Easy to Know

Sometimes it is easy to know God's grace. We have all been there when life is sailing, when dreams are realized, when we are feeling fulfilled with meaning and purpose. As my friend

Herb Barks puts it, "It's not that we *find* grace—grace searches for us."

At other times God's grace is not so easy to know.

So there is light—not enough to eliminate the darkness, but enough to illuminate our way through the darkness.

We have all been there, too, when life is difficult, or even tragic. Where is God's grace in the hard times? That's the question.

A husband dies after fifty-two years with his wife.

A young mother braces for her oncologist's report.

A much-needed job is lost.

A spouse learns of her partner's infidelity.

A man in his seventies, diagnosed with Alzheimer's, begins the slow goodbye and struggles to recall his grandchildren's names.

A mother innocently picks up the phone and learns of her daughter's accident.

For no reason, one morning an infant doesn't awaken.

Where is God's grace then? Sometimes it's not so easy to know. It's a piece of cake to see grace when we are flying high, but what about the times when we ache? Where is God's grace when we have to say goodbye to someone who means as much to us as life itself? Or say goodbye to a marriage or a dream or a purpose? In these circumstances can we really know God's presence, nearness, and grace? Really?

Yes. The short answer is *yes*.

Our Awareness of God's Presence

We turn to the promises of our faith. We look for grace in the times of darkness. We look for those glimpses of light that shine in the dark. In the middle of our dark nights of the soul, John's words come back to us, "The light shines in the darkness, and the darkness did not overcome it" (John 1:5). The light is the Presence that sustains us and guides us.

No, the light doesn't eliminate the darkness, the loneliness, the hurt—how we wish it did. But we weren't promised floodlights. Theologian and writer Frederick Buechner said it well, "In the darkness of a church, the candles burn. They hold the darkness back, just barely hold it back."[1]

So there is light—not enough to *eliminate* the darkness, but enough to *illuminate* our way through the darkness. We are never beyond the reach of God's grace. Even as we struggle, we are blessed with the grace of God's presence.

To those who have never been there, "the awareness of God's presence" may sound rather limp and passive. It is not. If you want to know the power of presence just find yourself in a hospital waiting room worried and anxious about your spouse who is now in surgery. You helplessly wait. A friend walks in to join you, hands you a cup of coffee, and waits with you for the duration. At times you talk about the surgery, then casual events of the day, and often there is the quiet of friends for whom conversation is not always needed. Through the anxious day together you feel support and compassion in her soothing company. You sense the grace of presence.

God waits with us—if we allow ourselves to be open to God's presence in the moment.

Please hear these too-rarely quoted words of Isaiah:

When you pass through the waters, I will be with
  you;
    and through the rivers, they shall not overwhelm
    you;
when you walk through fire you shall not be burned,
  and the flame shall not consume you. . . .
Because you are precious in my sight,
  and honored, and I love you. . . .
Do not fear, for I am with you.
—Isaiah 43:2-5

There will be rivers. Sooner or later we all will know the floods of grief, loss, and disappointment. You know we will. But we shall not be overwhelmed.

There will be fire. We will feel the heat of the pressures of life with its stress and anxiety. But we will not be consumed.

Why not? Because, God said, "I am with you." And why is God with us? "Because you are precious in my sight, and honored, and I love you."

God always has a resurrection beyond any of life's crucifixions.

Ten years ago, Karen was diagnosed with cancer. As she successfully fought it, God was with us every step of the way. Usually with his unobtrusive, quietly comforting "still small voice." At other times God seemed to speak more clearly.

Karen had major surgery following her diagnosis of breast cancer. Though it was a most difficult ordeal, she maintained her usual positive spirit. She believed that prayer, following good medical advice, and a positive attitude were the most important things she could do both in her recovery and in fighting cancer. Many times I heard her on the phone with friends— obviously following their question, "What can I do for you?"—and she would say, "Make me laugh." Many times I heard her response, "Make me laugh."

It had been almost a month after her surgery. The upcoming chemo and radiation had not yet begun. On a Saturday morning, I asked Karen if I could take her out for lunch. She had not been out of the house yet except for doctors' appointments. She said yes and picked her favorite Chinese restaurant.

We enjoyed our lunch together. The check came, with the fortune cookies. I broke mine open and read whatever it said. From across the table, I heard Karen laugh as she read hers. She handed it to me. With God as my witness, it said, "Laughter is the best medicine."

We each have been through our struggles, our heartaches— sometimes events have brought us to our knees. We intentionally have kept our faith in focus. We have whispered the passage, "[Nothing] will be able to separate us from the love of God in Christ Jesus our Lord" (Romans 8:35, 37-39).

Or maybe it was, "Remember, I am with you always" that best kept us grounded (Matthew 28:20). We are reminded of what ultimately matters. God and God's grace are here.

Happiness and Joy

The experience of God's presence, even in the times of struggle, offers a measure of peace and even joy. But please understand this is *joy*, not *happiness*. The distinction between the two is important. Our understanding of them often merges, which can get confusing.

> Happiness is emotional.
> Joy is spiritual.

> Happiness is from the heart.
> Joy is of the soul.

Happiness is emotional, and I'm all for it. It is our response when events around us are going well. I am happy when good happens to me. I am unhappy with the bad. Happiness is focused on the circumstances of my life and the events of the moment.

Joy looks through wide-angle lenses; it sees the big picture. Joy sees past the momentary. It senses the grace that is always present, whatever the events of life.

In times of heartache, by definition, I am *not happy*. But if my soul is right, if I have my spiritual bearings, if I am anchored in my awareness of God's presence, then, in spite of my unhappiness, I may well feel a peace, a confidence, a soulful grounding of grace—even *joy*.

God Creates Resurrections
Out of Life's Crucifixions

There is a second way we are blessed with God's grace through the tough times of our lives.

I came across a saying years ago that is profoundly true and has served me well: *"God can use what he didn't choose."* God can use for our benefit any life situation in which we find ourselves, though God would never have wanted it or chosen it for us. God can help us play any hand we are dealt. For, you see, *God always has a resurrection beyond any of life's crucifixions.*

First, an aside: How I wish God had put it all together differently. I have often said, with tongue firmly planted in cheek, if only God had consulted me when creating the world, I could have been *enormously* helpful!

Why the pain, the heartache? I have no idea. As a friend of mine said, "When I cross the Jordan I'm going with questions." God doesn't cause tragedy or pain; we know that. The mystery is why it is allowed in the world of his creation.

I often find myself with Job asking why. And, as with Job, God seems to look at me, working not to be sarcastic, and says, "Why are *you* questioning *me* about the meaning of life? Now just where were you when I created the mountains? Ron, don't worry about understanding it all. Don't worry; I have had it covered for a long, long time. Trust me."

And I do.

We not only can make it through our dark nights, we can come out the stronger for having been there. Heartache often will push us to depths we have never been before, to draw on resources we didn't know we had—and we return stronger, deeper, more substantial.

We have each known high points. I think of the elderly gentleman describing the years of his life: "My, but I have witnessed a grand parade." We have had some grand moments of spiritual and human experience. Yet, tucked in between those high moments, those peaks of experience, there have been valleys.

It is in these moments of our lives that God also speaks to us. In the good times he speaks clearly. In the times of struggle he speaks in a softer, more subdued voice. Years ago my friend and pastoral counseling colleague, Bob Gary, introduced me to the idea that the Creation story is really my story. Hear God's words from Scripture as spoken personally to you:

> In the beginning God created the heaven and the earth. And the earth was without form, and void; and darkness was upon the face of the deep. And the Spirit of God moved upon the face of the waters. And God said, Let there be light: and there was light. And God saw the light, that it was good: and God divided the light from the darkness. And God called the light Day, and the darkness he called Night. And the evening and the morning were the first day. (Genesis 1:1-5 KJV)

Whenever I hear that passage spoken personally to me, I get it. I think we all do.

We know about being "without form and void"—of times when our hopes crumbled, our plans upended, our direction sidetracked.

And we know too well of darkness, personal darkness—of stress or disappointment or unspeakable grief.

"And the world was without form, and void; and darkness was upon the face of the deep."

But the story continues. "And the Spirit of God moved upon the face of the waters." God's Spirit moved across the face of that darkened mass.

And God blessed it with a word of grace, "Let there be light: and there was light."

That must have been some truly pitiful-looking real estate. But God was looking through gracious eyes.

And what God saw in it, God called from it. God looked to that dark mass and said, "Let there be light." And creation began.

We not only can make it — we make it, having grown wiser and stronger.

Within every darkness, there is grace.

In my times of difficulty and turmoil, I remember. In the times my life is a mess, I remember the Spirit of God is moving over those waters. And God says, "Let there be light," and there will be light. And creation—maturity, growth, wisdom—begins.

Barbara Brown Taylor reminds us that God created both the day and the night—and placed treasures in both the light and in the darkness.[2] Strength, character, and insight are some of the treasures, some of the blessings of the night.

Make no mistake, these times before the dawn are difficult, painful, and often frightening. These are the experiences that bring many into my office saying, "My faith was really shaken by this." I understand, for God surely seemed utterly silent. Their prayers had gone unanswered. They felt alone. *Yet, in the darkness and through the turmoil, God quietly is at work—bringing light out of darkness, resurrection out of crucifixion.*

In each of our moments of *heartache*, God's grace is there as we grow in maturity, in character, in depth.

In periods of *stress* and *anxiety*, God's grace is there as we grow in knowledge, insight, and confidence in discovering our abilities under duress.

In times of *sin*, God's grace is there as we experience the awareness of separation and receive the blessing of humility, forgiveness, and reconciliation with God and with who we are created to be.

In experiences of *failure* and *disappointment*, God's grace is there as we gain wisdom, discernment, and judgment.

Julian of Norwich writes of our wounds as being "holes in the soul," where light and life can break through.

I think of times of struggle or grief or distress in my life as visits to a place I can only call my soul. I go there, as do you, and return . . . *changed*. We not only can *make it*—we make it, having *grown* wiser and stronger.

Theologian Gerald May said it well in his book *The Dark Night of the Soul*, "Each experience of the dark night gives its gifts, leaving us freer than we were before, more available, more responsive, and more grateful. . . . But they don't arrive until the darkness passes. They come with the dawn."[3]

> *You may well have prayed and prayed in those final months at home, then at hospice, for a miracle. Prayer after prayer, day after day, for a miracle. And then your mother died.*
>
> *Where was God? Where was God right there when you needed him? Where was that miracle when you so desperately wanted it?*
>
> *Later, between the waves of disappointment and grief, you reflected on those final months. The time together, as the clouds gathered, was precious. A special closeness was felt as you laughed and cried together, knowing that her fleeting life and your time together is a gift—always to be savored, never to be taken for granted. Heightened by your awareness of the beauty*

of those moments, you felt an intimacy that would always be with you for the rest of your life.

The time was such a precious gift, shared before the final goodbye. "Thank God," you said, "for that time, those moments, those days together. To have shared it was like . . . well, a miracle."

Some miracles, some moments of grace—some of God's finest—are right before our eyes.

We are stronger persons spiritually and emotionally for having been pushed by life circumstances to go where we never wanted to go. By the experience we are given strength, character, depth, and hope. This is what Paul meant when he wrote, "suffering produces endurance, and endurance produces character, and character produces hope, and hope does not disappoint us, because God's love has been poured into our hearts through the Holy Spirit that has been given to us" (Romans 5:3b-5).

Paul's insight is invaluable—suffering, endurance, and character bring hope.

Following any suffering, any heartache—if we will emotionally and spiritually engage it with endurance—a new depth of maturity and character may well emerge, and that brings confidence in who we are and hope for the journey ahead.

I came across the story of Neil Selinger, a successful New York attorney who retired in his mid-fifties to devote his time to serving his community and writing. He tutored at the high school and volunteered at the food pantry and Habitat for Humanity. He signed up for a class at the Writing Institute at Sarah Lawrence College and began writing his memoirs.

Soon after he began this new chapter of his life, he received the dreaded diagnosis of ALS, and his health began a sharp decline.

His writing teacher noted that as his physical abilities diminished, he gained a deeper sense of self. Neil was to write, almost poetically, in an unpublished essay, "As my muscles weakened, my writing became stronger. As I slowly lost my speech, I gained my voice. As I diminished, I grew. As I lost so much, I finally started to find myself."[4]

We all love to live in the light where we know laughter and happiness. We naturally resist difficulty. I think of the delightful card I once saw. The front of the card was addressed to "Dear whatever-docsn't-kill-you-makes-you-stronger." The message inside read, "I'm strong enough. Thank you."

We love the light, but it is usually in the darkness that we develop and mature. My most meaningful growth has come out of the darkness of struggle. Some lights can be seen, some grace can be known only in the darkness. Remember how the wise men were guided? They followed a star, a light they could see only in the darkness.

We are never beyond the reach of God's grace.

The Deepening Empathy

We return from our suffering having grown. Then there is a second grace. As we return with a new understanding of ourselves and of our lives, there is a deepening empathy transformed by the experience.

Poet Naomi Shihab Nye captured this beautifully in the opening words of her poem "Kindness."

> Before you know kindness as the deepest thing
>   inside,
> you must know sorrow as the other deepest thing.[5]

There is nothing like being with those who have *been there*. You see it in their eyes. They understand. They get it. *And* they feel for you and with you—from the empathy that was transformed and deepened by their own personal journeys into the darkness.

They are not just in your presence. They have joined you in your pain. Their paths and yours have merged for a time, and you walk together. You know in your soul that they have been here before. As Franciscan priest and author Richard Rohr wrote, "The real authority that 'authors' people and changes the world *is an inner authority that comes from people who have lost, let go, and are refound on a new level*."[6]

> *I sit in a counseling session with a mother whose daughter died tragically of childhood cancer. I listen to her as she pours out her pain. I listen to her. I hear her story. I may not be consciously thinking of my own son's death, but the awareness is back there. Somewhere in the background. Intuitively—without a conscious thought—I draw from those days many years ago when I walked a similar path.*
>
> *Be quiet.*
> *Listen.*
> *Be present.*
> *Care.*
> *Always, deeply care.*

CHAPTER 9

Our Response to Grace

We love because he first loved us.
—1 John 4:19

True compassion is a spirit that develops with intentional growth. It is not readily attained. It flourishes as we mature. It is like a plant that sprouts from a single seed that fell to the ground and took root. That seed, the origin of this emerging compassion, was a moment of inspiration we call grace.

First we receive the blessing,
then we become the blessing.

How then do we nurture this experience of grace? We first embody it. Grace becomes a part of who we are.

Remember our definitions of grace?

First, "the free and unmerited favor of God,"
then "a virtue coming from God."

First we receive the favor,
then the favor becomes a virtue.

First we receive grace,
    then we become gracious.

First we receive the blessing,
    then we become the blessing.

First we receive the compassion,
    then we become more compassionate.

Grace transforms us. We don't just do more gracious acts, we become more gracious as persons.

The experience of grace changes us into people who become something more than we were before—or, perhaps, *all* that we were before.

Having known God's own compassion for us, we are transformed into compassionate people. We are touched—and changed—by grace. Our acts of compassion will come as a natural result of this transformation—but let's not rush our focus on the deeds.

First, become fully aware of the change in you. You have been touched by grace.

For decades I have been moved by these words of theologian Paul Tillich: "You are accepted. You are accepted by that which is greater than you. . . . Do not try to do anything now; perhaps later you will do much. Do not seek for anything; do not perform anything; do not intend anything. *Simply accept the fact that you are accepted!*"[1]

You are loved.

Accept the fact that you are loved by the God of all creation. Allow that awareness to sink in.

Let it become a part of who you are.

"Laughter of the Heart"

I was talking with a friend who was going through the difficult experience of chemotherapy. I asked him about it, with my empathy at the ready, for I knew what a struggle this had been for him. And it was— but that wasn't his focus. After briefly acknowledging how rough it was, he said, and I paraphrase here:

> *"But, you know, I was sitting at the clinic the other day. I was in my chair all hooked up to the chemo, and I thought of all the people who sat in that chair in the years ahead of me. I thought of all the cancer patients on whom the doctors had learned what worked and what didn't. And I realized I am the beneficiary of their sacrifice.*
> *"I felt deeply blessed and thankful."*

A part of our transformation from lives that are blessed to lives that become a blessing is the experience of gratitude. Receiving "the free and unmerited favor of God" calls for sincere thankfulness, as would the reception of any such gift.

It is not surprising that from the Latin origin for *grace—gratia*—comes the word *gratitude*. When we receive grace, we experience gratitude. One naturally flows from the other. We are blessed first by the grace and then by the feeling of thankfulness. I love the way columnist David Brooks expressed this feeling, "Gratitude is a sort of laughter of the heart that comes about after some surprising kindness."[2]

There is at least a warmth, if not an exhilaration—yes, even a "laughter of the heart"—felt with gratitude.

Grace is relational. To receive grace without feeling thankful is to feel "lucky." To know grace as a gift implies a giver. To feel gratitude is to be thankful to the ones or the One by whom we are blessed.

When grace is known without a sense of thankfulness something has gone awry. Something is missing.

At first blush it seems ironic that those with difficult life journeys tend to be the most thankful for the blessings of the lives they have. After illness or heartache or struggle, blessings are no longer givens. They are no longer assumed. One's perspective is changed. A charmed life is no longer the baseline.

> *CNN News televised Lori Maville as she returned to her burned home after fire swept through her small town of Crest, California. What had been her home was totally destroyed. As the fire approached, she had hurried away not wearing her wedding ring. Now she stood in the ashes of what had been her bedroom looking, of course, for her ring.*
>
> *She looked, and she found it! The modest diamond was still in its setting. It could have been one of those overplayed, emotional television moments. But it wasn't. It was of a quiet, thoughtful woman standing there, in the middle of the rubble of what had been her life, looking at her wedding ring. She said softly, "It's a miracle."*
>
> *Ankle deep in ash, not even a wall standing, and that moment was declared "a miracle." It was. She still had the loving relationships that meant the world to her, and now she found the symbol of that love.*[3]

Many find that when life is stripped of what had been there in such abundance they refocus on the greater importance of the blessings that remain. Often these were the more important blessings all along. Each day then becomes a good day. They come out richer for the struggle.

Abundance is no longer assumed. It is received as a gift. And gratitude is felt.

To have been looked on with the gaze of divine grace, something changes within us and alters how we look to others.

Those who have lived with abundance all of their lives often struggle with feeling the grace with which they have been blessed. Blessings became givens in life. The bar of expectation of what life was to bring them was set too high.

Blessings are not blessings when they are expected, when they are assumed. Tragically, grace is then modestly experienced.

"The unmerited favor of God," is our first definition of grace. Unmerited.

Not expected.

Never assumed.

The blessings of life are all gifts, for which we are profoundly grateful.

It was noon, and the monks gathered in the dining room of the monastery to have lunch together. As they passed around the bread, which was particularly good, a monk tore off a piece and asked the one who had prepared the meal, "Did we make this bread or was it given to us?"

He answered, "Yes."

Life, with all its blessings, is grace. What we feel as we receive the gift is gratitude. And the circle continues.

Compassion as Our Response

To have been looked on with the gaze of divine grace, something changes within us and alters how we look to others. There is less judgment, less self-centeredness.

Replacing judgment is compassion, with its desire to support and care. Instead of self-centeredness there is loving-kindness, with its focus on the well-being of those we meet. Grace then takes on its human face.

> *I can just picture Jesus's gaze as he looked up. His sight was focused above the crowd and the noise and the turmoil. He looked up and saw the man in the tree. "Zacchaeus, hurry and come down; for I must stay at your house today" (Luke 19:5b). For one of the rare moments in his life, the man to whom Jesus spoke felt accepted and welcomed. He was invited into relationship. He felt grace.*
>
> *As he scurried down the sycamore, he had been transformed. "Look, half of my possessions, Lord, I will give to the poor; and if I have defrauded anyone of anything, I will pay back four times as much," he said (v. 8). Grace inspires graciousness. "Today salvation has come to this house," Jesus pronounced (v. 9). On that day, the grace Zacchaeus received and*

gladly shared became the center of who he had now become.

We receive the Gift.
    We are changed by the Gift.
        We offer the Gift.

This is the sequence. It comes full circle.

We complete the cycle by sharing, by serving. "The free and unmerited favor of God" then transforms into "a virtue coming from God," as we have defined grace.

There is a spiritual balance, a divine synergy at play. One follows the other. As Karl Barth wrote, "Grace must find expression in life, otherwise it is not grace."[4] Grace calls for more than a warm feeling—*grace calls for a response.*

Because God first loved us, we love. We are changed by what we have received. We have become something more.

We want to love.

PART III

Compassion of the Mind

CHAPTER 10

Standing Before Your Burning Bush

"If you choose, you can make me clean." . . . *Jesus stretched out his hand and touched him, and said to him, "I do choose."*
—Mark 1:40-41

The Rabbi stood before the children of his synagogue and asked, "What is the greatest day in Jewish history?"

A hand went up. "Moses leading the Israelites out of Egypt?" one asked.

"Good answer, but no."

"Moses bringing the commandments down from Mt. Sinai?"

"Another good answer, but I'm afraid not."

"The people of Israel crossing the Jordan to the Promised Land?"

"Yet another good try, but, again, no. No, the greatest day in Jewish history is . . . today."

And what is the greatest day in *human* history? Yes, today.

Yesterday the opportunity did not exist.

Tomorrow it will have passed.

Today is our day. Today is the greatest day in human history.

And the greatest moment in the greatest day in human history is *this* moment. Today is *your* day. This is *your* moment.

The seventeenth-century French Jesuit, Jean-Pierre de Caussade, said it well, "If we have abandoned ourselves to God, there is only one rule for us: the duty of the present moment."[1]

What does this moment ask of me?

That is our question—and for the answer we must listen with prayerful attention.

The hallmark of the "compassion of the mind" is *action*, doing what is right and caring. Its focus is not on the emotion or the motivation so much as *the will to live out our compassion*. We are "transformed by the renewal of [the] mind," is how Paul wrote it (Romans 12:2 NAB).

As we considered earlier, compassion of the heart is about the feeling, and from the soul springs the inspiration. From the mind comes the *will* and the *decision* to act. From the mind also comes the discernment on *how*, *where*, and *in what ways* to engage our compassion.

At the center of this compassion of the mind is what Jesus often referred to as *agape*. As we know, *agape* is the Greek word for love that emphasizes the priority to act on another's behalf. Unlike *eros* and *philia*, feelings are not the focus. We don't have to feel warm and fuzzy to get the loving job done. It's a plus, but it is not required.

As we love our neighbors—and, heaven knows, as we love our enemies—we are not called even to *like* them. Only to *love* them. To act on their behalf, for their welfare, because we love God.

Agape begins with a decision. It is intentionally deciding to extend ourselves beyond what benefits us.

Agape begins with what we do with that choice.

To Make a Choice

I have heard for years the debate over who we are as persons framed as "nature vs. nurture." Which is the greater influence, the discussion goes, the traits contained in our DNA or the influence of our parents and others during our childhood?

A strong case can be made on the "nature" side, of the role genetics plays in defining our core personality. So much of who we become is God-given and not developed.

I have read numerous studies over the years of identical twins who were separated at birth and adopted by different families. Though they were reared in totally different environments, their interests, personalities, preferences, and life directions had remarkable parallels. Clearly so much of who they were was on the genetic hard drive. The Scriptures spoke to DNA long before there were geneticists to give us the details. The prophet Jeremiah wrote, "Before I formed you in the womb I knew you" (Jeremiah 1:5).

Then there is the other view emphasizing *how one is reared* and nurtured.

Those with this perspective rightly point to the influence of those key figures in one's early years. "Train up a child in the way he should go," the Scriptures read, "and when he is old, he will not depart from it" (Proverbs 22:6 KJV). The guidance, support, caring—or the lack of it—will shape a person for the rest of his or her life. For better or worse, we are affected.

This brings us to what I think of as the third element in who we become. Nature and nurture are both powerful and important. But there is more. There is another determinant. It is displayed in the lives of those for whom genetics and upbringing do not account for all we see in the remarkable persons they become.

In the equation of who we are, the third element is *choice*.

We are, indeed, strongly influenced by our genes and our upbringing, but we are not bound by them. We may be limited by a lack of innate ability in certain areas—we may be able to go but so far, but we can choose to go *that* far. Do nature and nurture limit us? You bet. But we are far more limited by our lack of vision and motivation and self-discipline than by the constraints of nature and nurture. We can *choose* to bring our best. We can *decide* to bring our compassionate best.

Though nature and nurture are limiting, I think of them primarily as the foundations from which we grow into who we are to become. They are the foundations on which we make the choices that become our lives. In some ways, we are *bound* by them—in others our lives *abound* because of them.

We need and value all three. Together, they form who we are.

Our scriptural framework for this entire writing is from Jesus's response to the question of the greatest commandment. To love, he said, "with all your heart, and with all your soul, and with all your mind" (Matthew 22:37). With all our

Heart—which comes from *nurture*, as we are guided and taught;
Soul—which comes from *nature*, as God created us;
Mind—which comes from our *choices* over a lifetime.

I think of *nurture*—heart—as how we were reared.

It is the values we were taught and the countless lessons life has continued to model for us, mostly good (which we want to embrace), some dubious (which we need to evaluate), and others that are not "me" (which we let go).

And there is *nature*—soul—as our spiritual and emotional God-given core. This emotional DNA, with its strengths and weaknesses, abilities and disabilities, is the foundation to the persons who are uniquely us. Yet at the center of our souls is the *imago*, the image of the God placed within each of us, making every human life both precious and bursting with divine potential.

Then we have *choice*—which is of the mind.

In the midst of all the voices and directions and temptations competing for our attention, we ask: Which is the voice of God and to what is God calling us?

So it comes down to a simple, important question: *What shall we do with our choices?*

The nature and nurture chapters have been largely written, but I sit with pen in hand writing the current chapter based on *my* choices. Nature and nurture become almost irrelevant when it comes to focusing on the moment. I am not responsible for the first two. In fact, I had virtually no say whatsoever. But the third one is *totally in my hands.*

Whether life has dealt us an excellent hand or a notably weak one, we always have a choice. I think of a wise quotation often attributed to either Robert Louis Stevenson or Jack London: "Life is not a matter of holding good cards, but of playing a poor hand well."

We have no say on the raw materials life has handed us, but we have all the say on what we will do with them.

Choice comes in when we hear the voice of God calling for our best, and living with integrity insists that we follow it.

The choice is ours.

Moses heard God's voice. He then readily reminded God in the glow of the burning bush that nothing in his upbringing prepared him for the assignment he was now being given.

Wouldn't you have just loved to hear that debate? Moses is standing in the presence of the fire of God, hearing the very voice of God, and his response is "But . . . but . . . but. . . ."

If the decision is important (and we are wise) we go to a deeper place. We listen for a deeper voice.

"But Moses said to God" is recorded time after time in that single conversation detailed in the Book of Exodus. He was saying, "But, Yahweh, I don't think you really get it. I'm not your man. I honestly believe I've got nature *and* nurture working against me here. You need to burn another bush and find another guy."

However, God saw, as God does with most of us, more in Moses than Moses saw in himself. God called him to reach beyond the likely and answer with his best. And Moses responded. As Dumbledore says to his student Harry Potter in *The Chamber of Secrets*, "It is our choices, Harry, that show what we truly are, far more than our abilities."

Times of Decision

Compassion of the mind is first a choice.

We have to decide, as we live out our day, how we will respond in life's spontaneous moments to the human need with which we are faced.

A woman dressed in a worn sweater with two little girls in tow outside our grocery store says they haven't eaten all day and asks if we could help.

A coworker's husband has just been diagnosed with leukemia, she says, and she "just wanted us to know."

We step into our closets and see rows of clothes and shoes we haven't worn in ages, but we "might need them" one day, we think. Then we remember our community ministry's clothes closet . . .

Someone from the church calls and asks if we could lead a mission team to work on a school in Belize next spring.

We pause. Before we decide, we pause.

And in the moment, if the decision is important (and we are wise) we go to a deeper place. We listen for a deeper voice.

For decisions that need maturity and judgment, we don't want to react from ego or pride. For choices that call for thoughtfulness or compassion, we don't want to act on self-centeredness.

We want to respond from a deeper voice—one that is reflective, thoughtful, discerning.

The pause encourages us to slow down,
> to respond to the moment,
>> to the request,
>>> to the person,
>>>> with consideration and grace.

For years I have urged those who are impulsive in what they say—especially when angry—to pause and remember these words before they speak: *Respond, don't react.*

It only takes a second. But in that instant a harsh reaction can instead become a thoughtful response.

What happens in that brief, reflective pause is interesting. In the geography of the brain I *react* from the amygdala. It is in the limbic region and is the emotional part of the brain—often called "the lizard brain," since we share it with all animals. As the reactive region, it is the center of the "fight or flight" response. It comes out raw and usually self-serving.

In the momentary pause of "respond, don't react" we intuitively shift from the amygdala to the prefrontal cortex, known as the executive functioning part of the brain.

In that instant, we begin to balance the raw emotion with thoughtfulness and respect. We begin to integrate our sensitivity and our values into *how* we will respond. Though we are the same persons responding—as the ones who would have been reacting—we are *now* relating from a thoughtful place.

As we apply this same phrase, "respond, don't react," to the context of compassionate decisions, we slow down the process.

We pause.

We reflect.

To what do I feel called at this moment of my life?
What shall I decide?
More broadly, how is this day to be invested?
How is my life to be used?

The question echoes from the Scriptures, "And who knows whether you have not come to the kingdom for such a time as this?" (Esther 4:14 ESV).

For what is this my time?

By pausing, by responding from a place of reflection and discernment, not only do I not respond from my amygdala, I am not even responding entirely from my prefrontal cortex.

For matters that involve compassion I am also responding from my heart, if not from my soul.

Charles Dickens begins his novel *David Copperfield* with the words, "Whether I shall turn out to be the hero of my own life, or whether that station will be held by anyone else, these pages must show."[2]

Whether we shall turn out to be the woman or man God created and called us to be, the choices we make as we are writing these pages of our lives—today—will show.

CHAPTER 11

Compassion and Service

"For the Son of Man came not to be served but to serve."
—Mark 10:45

Service. About this point Jesus was clear and unambiguous.

"Do you love me?" *Then feed my sheep.*
"Do you love me?" *Then roll up your sleeves.*
"Do you love me?" *Then here is a basin and a towel.*
"Do you love me?" *Good. Be there.*

Compassion always becomes service—or it isn't really compassion.

It was one of the coldest days of the winter. I was at the Barnes & Noble bookstore just down the street. I got my coffee at the adjoining Starbucks and was walking through the bookstore past the magazine rack. As I made the turn at the end of the rack where they stack the Sunday newspapers, I almost stepped on a man. He was kneeling in front of the stack of Atlanta papers.

I looked down and saw a homeless man on his knees looking intently at the morning paper. He had several sections folded back.

As I looked more closely, it almost took my breath away—he was looking intently on this bitterly cold day at the weather page. I stopped in my tracks. There knelt a homeless man looking at the weather page. He was looking at the paper just as I would look at my thermostat—for that is the world in which he lived.

On Outreach Sunday one year our pastor said, "You can go to all the Bible studies you want to, you can raise all the hands you want to raise, you can praise Jesus all day, but if it doesn't carry you into the street where people are hurting, then that faith is of absolutely no value."

Service. *Compassion always becomes service—or it isn't really compassion.*

To serve is to set aside our tasks and agendas and be responsive to the needs and welfare of others. It is to extend ourselves beyond ourselves to those who need us.

Service is not about us. It is not to impress anyone or to feel good about ourselves or to look good. It is not even to *be good* so much as to *be faithful*—faithful to the call we feel deeply within in response to the grace we have known. *When compassion is felt, service is not an obligation—it's a given.* We could not do otherwise.

Something would be missing in the equation of our lives without service.

Remember that balance between *receiving* the blessing and *becoming* the blessing? Without becoming a blessing something important would be left out. Something within our hearts, within our souls, would be empty.

It's like an invitation left on the kitchen counter to which we never responded. When we do not attend the event, we are left with an emptiness from having missed out.

Service is the second grace. The first is to be loved. The second is to be loving. Albert Schweitzer put it this way, "I don't know what your destiny will be, but one thing I know: the only ones among you who will be really happy are those who will have sought and found how to serve."[1]

Compassion for the Least

I am reminded of the moment when Jesus was approached by the leper.

Leprosy in those days was not just the rare skin disorder we know as leprosy today. It was a broad term that included common skin diseases that would cover a person's body, for which there are treatments today.

Day after day the lepers hid from view. When walking in public they called out, "Unclean, unclean." People viewed them with a combination of disgust and fear, moving as far away as they could. They were reviled, even though they had done nothing.

They were never to hear a kind word. Never to know the compassion of another's touch. The loneliness. The isolation. We talk about self-esteem problems—we haven't a clue compared to the daily humiliation of their lives.

This was the context on that day as this man with leprosy chose not to walk on the far side of the street. Instead, he walked right through the crowd. They scattered like a covey of quail getting away from him.

He walked up to Jesus. On his knees he said, "If you choose, you can make me clean." Jesus said, "I do choose."

Underline that sentence. I do choose.

To love—agape—is a choice.

And then came the moment: Jesus reached out his hand. Such a simple thing. But a simple thing that no one standing there had ever seen before. He reached out his hand, and he touched the man with leprosy.

Without a doubt, there was a gasp from the crowd. "Be made clean!" he said, and the man was healed (Mark 1:41-42).

But, excuse me, I can't take my eyes off the *first* miracle. Not the one that healed his body but the one that healed his *heart*.

Someone had the compassion to touch him. He now knew he was no longer a "leper." He was a man of dignity and value, worthy of being touched, who happened to have leprosy.

All of that was spoken in Jesus single, simple gesture of reaching out his hand.

When our daughter, Brooke, was almost three, she had two imaginary playmates. To our surprise, they were Cinderella's nasty stepsisters, Anastasia and Drizella. These stepsisters would go with us everywhere we went.

Karen and I waited as long as we could without asking the obvious question. Finally, Karen asked her, "Brooke, your imaginary playmates are Cinderella's stepsisters, aren't they?"

"Yes, ma'am."

"As I recall, they aren't very nice girls, are they?"

"Oh, no ma'am."

"Then, Honey, why are they your playmates?"
"Well, Mama, they're the ones who need love the most."

The Gift of Your Nearness

Read the following words of the psalmist, and see if, through them, God whispers to you something of what I think I heard.

I will rejoice and be glad in Your lovingkindness,
Because You have *seen* my affliction;
You have *known* the troubles of my soul.
       —Psalm 31:7 NASB (emphasis added)

The psalmist is saying: When I have troubles, to be *seen* and to be *known* is the loving-kindness I need. For that I will rejoice.

To be seen, to be known—to be given the honor of your company. For that I will rejoice.

Service begins with who you are. Then with what you do.

At our church, we have an event called the Great Day of Service on the last Saturday in March each year. About nine hundred of us spread out over the city and work with agencies that serve those in need. We go to be with those who lead lives we can only imagine. We have not known hunger apart from a diet, or homelessness that didn't involve a camping trip. And, perhaps as important, we don't know what it is like to be invisible—to have people walk past us as if we were never there.

As important as anything we do is *to see and to know*—to care enough to engage others with warmth and sensitivity. It is to show the care and thoughtfulness that springs from a heart of compassion.

You may not have a formal event like the Great Day of Service—but, then again, of course you do. *Every* day of service is a great day.

> *You may volunteer at a place in your community for those who have fallen to the depths because of their addiction to alcohol or drugs and are courageously engaged in a program for recovery.*
>
> *You may meet a man there who had a good life—family, job, friends—before vodka became his companion and alcohol his addiction. Substance and alcohol abuse took over that good life and left him without a marriage or a family or even a place to sleep at night. He was sliding—farther and farther down—until the recovery center you visit stopped the slide and gave him a foothold.*
>
> *The recovery program offered him a start, a way to begin his long climb back. He is working hard to make the most of this opportunity. Shake his hand, as I know you will, with the firmness of one who honors him for what he has done and what—day by day—he works to continue to do.*
>
> *He needs you. In that brief, personal moment you will give him the two things in the shortest supply in his life . . . dignity and respect.*
>
> *In your eyes, he will know that he is not invisible. He will know that he is seen and known. You have shared with him the gift of grace.*

Or, perhaps, your personal ministry will take you to visit women who are imprisoned. You may well meet a woman who will readily acknowledge, in her words, it was her "own stupid fault" that she is there.

But there she is. And there she has been. And there she will be.

For seven years she has not watched her children grow up—has not even seen them except on visitation days. She can tell on those days her baby boy, now eight, doesn't really know her as his mother. Can you imagine? She will not see her daughter off on her first date or watch her graduate from high school or be escorted to that special pew for her wedding or take care of her and the grandbaby the first week home from the hospital.

The guilt, the loneliness, the ache only a mother could know.

She needs you. She feels like such a failure, and in the grace of your smile she may see a mirror and know she is a woman of worth and value. The respect in your voice, the encouragement of your company, are the affirmations she needs to make it through today.

Service begins with who you *are*. Then with what you *do*.

How Will I Serve?

Compassion means that we *want* to serve. Compassion then wonders *how* we will serve.

This is what Paul wrote in his words to the church in Philippi, "And this is my prayer, that your love may overflow more and more with knowledge and full insight to help you determine what is best" (Philippians 1:9-10).

This is precisely what I mean by "the compassion of the mind." In order to determine *what is best* in how our *love may overflow*, we engage the wisdom of *knowledge and full insight*.

There are countless ways we can serve, but some are far more effective in meeting needs and making a difference than are others. For example, when we give to charitable organizations after a natural disaster, some agencies will give much more of each dollar to the intended recipient than will others.

As we determine how we will serve, we want to know how our time and energy is best put to use in effectively meeting needs. Our intent is not just to feel good because we have given of ourselves. No, it is to feel good because we have *done* good in meaningful and substantial ways.

We must bring our knowledge and full insight about ourselves. "In what ways do you feel called to serve?" is the question.

Thoughtfully, reflectively, and prayerfully we consider *how* we want to offer ourselves. "Now there are varieties of gifts, but the same Spirit; and there are varieties of services, but the same Lord," wrote Paul (1 Corinthians 12:4-6). We will want to be intentional about matching the gifts we bring with the opportunities for service before us.

The value of discerning the match of *gifts* and *needs* is that the service tends to be more meaningful and lasting. We tend to stay longer in doing the work, in being involved in missions where we discover purpose and fulfillment.

There are three components involved for service to be meaningful and lasting. We need to look for a match where:

> *our ability* and
>> *a sense of call* lead us to
>>> *a meaningful need.*

Ability. We must bring an ability to do the task at hand.

This will vary in its importance, given the job to be done. Perhaps you don't bring the skill set but are willing to learn. I remember attending a meeting at The Carter Center here in Atlanta and hearing one of the center interns, upon completing his internship, say, "I came here wanting to care. I leave here knowing how."

We must also be "cut out for the job," both in terms of needed expertise and personality. If the task is not a fit for you, then you will be looking at the clock, and your service will be limited and of short duration.

A sense of call. We can do lots of things. But where do you feel a tug? In what direction in the offering of yourself do you sense a pull? What energizes you? What interests you—or even excites you?

> *I overheard my wife, Karen, say to someone on the phone who had just asked her to consider taking an office in our church for the coming year that she would like to think it over and call her back the next day. As she later said to me, "I wanted to give it twenty-four hours for the compliment to fade and then decide if it was a job I actually wanted to do."*

I am reminded of the parable of the talents (Matthew 25:14-30).

In our language, the concept of talents can be misleading. Though we know better, it is difficult not to associate the word *talent* with our English meaning of "ability." So we feel guilty as we sit in the congregation, with a lovely singing voice, aware that we are not in the choir. Or, with the proven ability to lead, we feel the shame that we didn't want to chair the board that does so much good in our community.

Back to the parable. A talent in this story isn't an ability. It is a denomination of money. It is a metaphor.

It is an ability *combined with a call*, a pull to use that ability in a certain direction. An ability plus a call gives you a direction for the investment of your talent—from which the return will be abundant.

Where you feel called is where you will find meaning.

Where you find meaning is where you will feel an urge to return, because there is a sense of God-given purpose. It is there that you will know the joy in service.

A meaningful need. Service is not busy work. It is not being a do-gooder or filling some imaginary quota or living out an image for our reputations. It is about meeting meaningful needs.

If the need is not truly one that feeds a stomach or clothes a child or touches a heart or does something that matters, then it may not be worth the investment of our time and energy. Our ability and our call are to be invested in needs that make a difference. If not, then something precious—the only lives we have—will have been wasted.

CHAPTER 12

Compassion and Boundaries

For everything there is a season, and a time for every matter
under heaven . . .
a time to embrace, and a time to refrain from embracing;
a time to seek, and a time to lose . . .
a time to keep silence, and a time to speak.
—*Ecclesiastes 3:1, 5b, 6a, 7b*

The parable of the good Samaritan has long been useful to me in understanding another dimension of compassion.

We know the story by heart. A man is traveling from Jerusalem to Jericho, and a gang attacks him, leaving him robbed and beaten. A couple of locals walk by, not wanting to get involved. Then a foreigner from Samaria comes along, sees the man, and kneels beside him. He cleans and bandages his wounds. He puts the man on his donkey and carries him into town.

End of story. It's about compassion. Go and do likewise.

Right?

Of course not. We know it's *not* the end of the story—it's just the place most tend to stop in the telling of the account.

The parable continues. The Samaritan takes the wounded man to an inn in town. He explains the situation to the innkeeper and gets him a room. He tends to the man's needs for the rest of the day. The next morning, he tells the innkeeper he has to be on his way and asks him to continue the care this man needs. He then pays for their stay, promising to stop by again when he is next in town to settle up with the innkeeper with any more he may owe him.

Boundaries are not about limiting how much we love—but how we love.

The Samaritan is then on his way.

The first half of the story is about *compassion*. The second half is about *boundaries*.

Those who are sincerely seeking to live out their faith will sometimes ask, "How much is enough?" How much am I to give? After all, we follow one who gave everything and was quoted as saying, "Love one another as I have loved you."

This can be troubling. My pitiful offering begins to look pretty modest in this context. And it is.

Boundaries are not about limiting how much we love. If we are spiritually living out of the Source of divine grace then our entire lives are to be about love. To love God and neighbor as self becomes the frame of reference for our lives. It will never be lived perfectly, but for persons of faith it is lived intentionally. To love becomes what we are about.

So boundaries are not about limiting how *much* we love— but *how* we love.

We need direction and focus in our compassion in order to do what is purposeful and sustainable. Otherwise—and let's be candid here—we will burn out and give up. We give our all, from the depths of our hearts, and healthy boundaries allow us to be back the next day to give our all again from the depths of our hearts.

We have restraints of time and energy and expertise affecting how much we have to give. No matter how much heartfelt passion we feel about addressing a need, these restraints are the realities that must be factored into what we can offer. It would be naive—and unwise—to ignore our limitations.

In this real world we each have these limitations on how we share the compassion we offer. We have lives of responsibilities and commitments.

We want to give more, but like the Samaritan, after a time, we have to be on our way and about our business.

> *Fresh out of seminary, I spent the first several years of my ministry as a parish pastor.*
>
> *I was fortunate to be a part of a consultation group for ministers during that time led by Carlyle Marney, a seasoned and respected veteran of our profession. He once asked us to share with the group the story of the parishioner with whom we had the most trouble connecting—to see how the group might be able to help.*
>
> *I knew who that would be. I told Marney and the group of the many times and ways I had reached out to this church member as her pastor—and of the many times and ways my attempts had been rebuffed. In a classic passive-aggressive style, she could find a way to include in most conversations with me how my predecessor had always engaged his ministry*

so beautifully. Hope against hope I trudged on and would try again.

I shared this story with the group and awaited their consultation. Marney, in his delightful drawl, said, "Well, you've worked awfully hard with this one." He paused and then leaned toward me and continued, "Now, Ron, you Methodists—every four or five years—don't you run one pastor out of a parish and bring another one in?"

"Something like that, Marney," I said.

"Well, Ron, let somebody else bless her."

Let somebody else bless her. Every human need is not ours to take on.

For the compassionate person, this may be a tough pill to swallow. It goes against the grain of every caring instinct we have.

We are to be boundless and *boundary-less* if we are truly compassionate. Right? I'm afraid not. To love without boundaries is true as a *feeling* but not as a *fact*. Our love is as boundless as the Source of our love, but how we live it out is done with judgment and discernment. We must refine our understanding of healthy compassion to include parameters if our loving-kindness is to be both effective and lasting.

As we are being compassionate, we also need to be wise.

There is a valued saying that goes, "The only difference between a river and a swamp is the river has boundaries." If my service is to have a productive flow, it can't be spread in all directions. How we devote ourselves in dedicated service has to have appropriate perimeters if it is to be meaningful.

Setting your boundaries means, first, guiding the flow of your compassion to where it can be meaningfully felt. There is only so much of each of us to give. We channel the time and energy we have into ways that matter, into causes that make a difference, and relationships with whom we connect. We must be selective.

Though we have focused on this earlier, here are the questions that seem most relevant to me as we decide where our focus will be:

To *what do I feel called?*
    What need inspires me to get involved?
        To *what arena of service does my mind and heart return?*
            To *what do I feel an enthusiasm about engaging?*
Where is the need the greatest?
    Where can my service offer the greatest impact?
        Where can I offer myself in a way that will also be meaningful to me?

These are the kinds of questions that may help us translate the emotion of caring into the reality of the world in need.

The needs around us are abundant. Which are yours to fill? In which arena of need do you want to invest this day of your life?

Boundaries of Commitment

So, we pause. We discern. And we decide in what arena we will commit our time, our attention, and our energy. Or perhaps we keep our radar on for the opportunity that feels right to us. When it comes along, we will seize it. We will commit.

Yet we commit thoughtfully. We have busy lives with responsibilities and obligations and aspirations. Perhaps, of course, we are too busy. We pause. We reflect on how we spend our days, on what we invest our time and our energy. We may be in need of a schedule renovation.

Step back and give it some thought periodically. Do you have your life as closely in balance with the priorities you have set as you possibly can? Then tweak what you need to tweak.

Given the realities and limitations of our world, we commit to the degree we are available. And there we draw our boundaries. I encourage you to feel good about both.

Feel good about the commitment, and feel good about the boundary.

Remember, the boundary keeps the river of your compassion flowing without spreading out in ways that are too broad and exhausting. If we take on too much, we are doing no one any favors. We will be, at best, tired and less effective, and at worst, bitter and resentful. There will always be more to do—but only so much of you to go around.

Set healthy limits. It is one of the most caring things you can do for those you serve.

Commitments for a Season

There are seasons to our lives. There are commitments we make for a lifetime, but most we make for a season. The commitment to many tasks or organizations may be important and meaningful, but they are only for a chapter of our lives.

We invest ourselves. We develop relationships. We work passionately. We give gladly and generously.

Then, as time passes—hours, months, years, even decades—we feel it. We know we have done what we came to do. It's time to turn the page. We begin the transition and turn ourselves to the engagements of the chapter that follows.

In our understanding of the story of the good Samaritan, in any commitment of service the question will sooner or later emerge: At what point will I have arrived at the inn?

At what point in my service have I done what I was called to do and now need to clear the way for others to make their contributions? We can't lose touch with our humility and forget that we bring only our talents to the task and, as we move on, we clear the way for others to bring theirs—and our place of service is the richer for it.

"Is it caring?" needs to be balanced by "Is it wise?"

So, when is that moment in time for you to move on?

I don't know.

But if you listen to your heart, you will.

Artists who work in oils and acrylics tell me there is a moment in every painting that the work is finished. In these two mediums, of course, they could paint forever, layer upon layer. But with a certain stroke of the brush the painting is completed.

Until that point, more was needed; but to continue to paint following that moment, the painting would be overdone and diminished. It is a part of the artistry *to know when that moment has come,* to know when the work is finished.

"It is finished," were also the words of Jesus from the cross (John 19:30).

Theologians debate whether *finished* meant that his earthly life was over or that his mission was completed. I think it was the latter. In ways small and large, we can understand.

Boundaries of Responsibility

We also set boundaries that respect the integrity of what is our responsibility and what is the responsibility of another.

In an earlier writing, I made the distinction between "caring for" and "taking care of" someone. To *care for* others is to do for them what they cannot do for themselves. To *take care of* them is to do what they can do—or have the ability to learn to do—for themselves. Between the two is where the boundary is to be drawn.

I am obviously a big fan of caring for others, since it's the heart of compassion. You and I gladly do for others what they cannot do for themselves—but we draw the boundary at what they can do.

I am glad to support and encourage them, but I will not step over the line and make their decisions for them or do what is their responsibility to engage. As the authors of *Boundaries* wrote, "We are to *love* one another, not *be* one another. . . . I can't think for you. . . . I can't grow for you; only you can."[1]

The importance of this boundary is multifaceted.

If I neglect to honor it I unnecessarily spend time and energy doing what they could do for themselves, which is no big deal.

But what is a big deal is that I may well *dishonor those I am intending to help*. My attitude in taking over their lives implies how little I think of their abilities. It is demeaning and condescending. But even worse, my well-intended-but-poorly-thought-through approach is potentially damaging to their sense of self-worth and may encourage dependency.

We have to be insightful. Just because we are filled with compassion, and this *feels* good, doesn't mean it *is* good for the recipients of our care. *If the only gain in this interaction is that*

I am left feeling good about myself, then the moment has fallen drastically short of the definition of compassion.

If we are being truly compassionate, we pause, step outside ourselves, and look at what we are about to do from the perspectives of those we are serving. Am I serving in a way that truly helps them and leaves them with a feeling of dignity and worth?

This is about compassion of the mind. We are intentional. We are thinking it through. We are engaging our insight and wisdom.

In the Hippocratic oath, in the midst of all the ideals to which physicians aspire, is the single, simple phrase setting the "low bar," below which they should never fall: "do no harm." In all the good to which we aspire, we must be mindful and attentive to avoid unintentional harm.

"Is it caring?" needs to be balanced by "Is it wise?"

An excellent discussion of this topic is in Robert Lupton's book *Toxic Charity*. He highlights several concerns in the ways many charities historically have served the poor. Often the handout method of charity leaves the recipients with an initial feeling of inferiority and humiliation. Then, over time—insult to injury—it encourages an attitude of dependency and entitlement.[2]

Lupton engages our "compassion of the mind," with its insight and wisdom, and develops strategies in which those who are poor can be given the gift of dignity in *how* compassion is offered. Instead of being given food and clothing, which can be demeaning, they are invited to *buy* them at a co-op at a fraction of the cost.[3] The emotional result for the receiver is empowerment and independence.

Insight and wisdom are vital ingredients in this whole recipe of compassion. As we see, loving-kindness is not just of the heart and soul—but also of the mind.

CHAPTER 13

Compassion Toward Ourselves

"You shall love your neighbor as yourself."
—Matthew 22:39

I mentioned in an earlier chapter that I read to patients at Hospice Atlanta. It is as meaningful as anything I do, beyond my family and my ministry. I began doing this out of a hunch that many of the patients love to read as much as I do but, because of their illness or medication, are no longer able to do so. That hunch proved to be true, and I became their eyes to whatever literature they enjoyed.

My visits at hospice also gave me the opportunity to sit and quietly chat with those on the threshold of the most important transition of their lives. I was not there as a counselor, simply a volunteer who came to read—and didn't mind lingering, sitting with them for a while longer so they wouldn't be alone.

Karen's cancer returned a handful of years ago. Her oncologist referred to it as "chronic" this time, meaning it may not be going away. This motivates us to seize every moment for all the joy and fulfillment we can find.

Karen takes her meds, gets her markers checked, and periodically has her scans. The nurse called on a Thursday. The report from the latest scan wasn't particularly good. It was not alarming, but there were new spots on her bones and lymph glands.

"Thank you for calling," Karen said, "and have a good afternoon."

We sat together and talked. We were not upset by the news. Just concerned. It had let the wind out of our sails.

We talked about our upcoming trip to Disney World several months down the road, taking our kids, their spouses, and the grands. Karen wanted to make sure she was going to be up to it.

The next day I got in the car to drive to hospice to read to the patients. I guess I felt a voice within my soul more than I actually heard one.

"No. Not now. This is not the time," is what I heard.

I knew as I continued the familiar drive that this would be my last visit for a good while. I did not need to be sitting with patients who were living out the very story Karen and I most feared. I needed to take better care of myself than come face-to-face with such a personal reminder, and the patients needed someone who was there without reservation. I drove on to hospice to say my goodbye.

The following Friday I honored a different commitment I had made several weeks before.

I sat in a rocking chair in my oldest grandson's second-grade class and read to a group of excited seven- and eight-year-olds the tales of The Gruffalo, The Highway Rat, *and* Jack and the Flumflum Tree.

I had transitioned into a new genre of literature and in a new setting that better fit this chapter of my life.

A Life in Balance

Earlier we considered the balance from John's letter, "We love because he first loved us." Because he first loved us, we love.

It is a healthy spiritual response. It's a life in balance. One follows the other, and if our lives are in order both are felt. If we only receive without serving, we become self-absorbed and entitled. If we only serve without receiving—and this is far more rarely seen—we soon wear out.

We need a life in balance.

When Jesus spoke of love of neighbor and love of self in the same breath, he meant that both are good.

Victor Frankl, the renowned psychiatrist and author of *Man's Search for Meaning*, spoke of a parallel balance of freedom with responsibility. He proposed that the Statue of Liberty on the east coast be supplemented by a Statue of Responsibility on the west coast.

I think of the synergy of our balance similarly—the pendulum swinging between receiving grace on one side and living graciously on the other.

There is a flow to this way of living. It is the flow I have attempted to describe in this writing as *springing from the soul, to inspire the heart, directed by the mind.* The pendulum swings in its rhythmic way from the blessing of the soul to the compassion of the heart, from the receiving to the offering. It is to tend to our own needs in preparation for tending to the needs of others. Both are required for the flow to be sustained.

> *Remember the story from the last chapter of John's Gospel of the resurrected Jesus having breakfast with the disciples on the shore?*
>
> *It was there he took Simon Peter and stepped away from the group. He looked him in the eyes and asked three times, "Simon son of John, do you love me?" Three times Peter affirmed his love. Each time Jesus responded with a form of "Feed my sheep" (John 21:15-17).*
>
> *Every time I have read this passage over the years I have done what most of us do. As Jesus took Peter aside, I identify with the disciple and feel Jesus's hand on my shoulder, "Ron, do you love me?" "Yes, Lord," I whisper. And I'd start looking for some sheep to feed.*
>
> *Then with one reading it struck me: Jesus didn't take me aside—he took Simon Peter. I'm not Simon Peter; I'm one of the sheep!*
>
> *"Simon son of John, do you love me?"*
>
> *"Yes, Lord."*

"Then feed my sheep—especially the tall one with the glasses over there."

In the first half of the balance we receive. Only then will we be ready to offer. Decide that it is all right to take good care of yourself. Realize that Jesus really meant it when he spoke of us having lives in all abundance.

When he spoke of love of neighbor and love of self in the same breath, he meant that both are good. As author Frederick Buechner wrote, "Take good care of yourself so you can take good care of them. A bleeding heart is of no help to anyone if it bleeds to death."[1]

Many who are inclined to serve find they struggle with the notion of caring for themselves. As it has been said, "If most of us 'loved our neighbors as ourselves' we'd be arrested." Let's face it, we can do this one really poorly. We are to love ourselves with the same care and attention we would offer a friend.

What's Going On?

Whenever we press too hard and take on too much we over-extend ourselves, which hurts us as well as those around us.

Do the obvious:

Set limits.
Prioritize.
Take time away.

If you find you can't make yourself set boundaries and say no, then you need to ask what you are getting out of saying yes.

What's going on?

What needs of yours are being met? Is there something you are trying to prove? Is the drive to serve without limits a kind of self-validation? Is there a self-image you are working to achieve? Are you trying to earn respect in the eyes of others— or yourself?

Let's be candid. We always have mixed motives. At our most compassionate moments there is a part of our motivation that is self-serving. We can never fully check our ego at the door. To some degree, it always comes in with us. It is a part of the human condition that our self-serving pride accompanies us, whatever we do.

How do we look? What impression are we making? How are we coming across? What does this do to our image? This gets pretty embarrassing, because it's true. It *is* true, and we need to recognize that it is—so we can keep it in check and address these needs on their own terms, not by excessive displays of service.

Self-service isn't our intention as persons who want to be compassionate—so we must be aware of it. We are not to be ashamed of it, simply aware of it.

When we feel fatigue instead of meaning at the thought of serving, we need to become reflective about what needs to change.

Only then can we best return to the goal of what we are about. We are called for a higher purpose. As our motivation we stay in touch with our ego and self-centeredness and insecurities and defenses to know when they are looming too large.

Discern. Wonder. When compassion fatigue sets in, you should wonder if some of these less-worthy motivations are too prominent and are leaving you drained.

> *An elderly clergy once said, "When I was young I sought to change the world. As I grew older, I limited it to my community. Now that I am older and wiser, I see that I should begin with myself."*

If you are experiencing compassion fatigue, do your inner work to discover what is going on and then address it in healthy ways—not by wearing yourself out in service.

Remember that when your compassion becomes compulsive, something besides compassion is motivating you. It needs to be discerned and addressed to free you to care from the heart.

What Needs to Change?

Even healthy compassion can be tiring.

When we care, we give. When we give, we are blessed, but we may also be weary. Compassion fatigue is seen when our compassion begins to feel more like a duty than a desire. What has gone awry for most of us is that this receiving and giving flow has stopped up, often on the receiving end—and we need to tend to the care of ourselves.

When we feel fatigue instead of meaning at the thought of serving, we need to become reflective about what needs to change. If our motive has become less about *offering from our abundance* and more about doing what we are *supposed to do,* then we have lost the balance, the flow.

Self-compassion is rapidly replacing *self-esteem* in therapeutic professional writing as the most significant factor in our emotional well-being.

Self-esteem is often determined comparatively—as we contrast ourselves, higher or lower, to others. The focus tends to be on success, ability, or attractiveness. It doesn't lend itself to healthy self-acceptance.

Develop your community.
Get rest.
Pray and meditate daily.
Practice gratitude.
Be true to who you are.

For some, the result is a self-righteous narcissism toward themselves and a kind of condescension toward others.[2] For others, who don't feel their self-identity fares well in the comparison, they live with a self-critical spirit and a level of depression that saps life of vitality and energy.[3]

Self-compassion, on the other hand, is not a valuation or score we give ourselves but something we do for ourselves— which turns out to be a better predictor both of increased happiness and optimism and of lower depression and anxiety.[4] Self-compassion frees us from the comparisons where we are better or lesser than others. It encourages us to befriend ourselves. We then can strive for excellence but with an inner voice of kindness instead of criticism.

This idea of self-compassion is to relate to ourselves *without* judgment and *with* grace.

This is not some silly version of singing "Kumbaya" to ourselves. It is to acknowledge our weakness and our failures without the kind of self-judgment that tends to shut us down and leave us least able to address those shortcomings creatively and constructively. Self-compassion brings an attitude of warmth and empathy, which acknowledges our struggles as being a part of the human condition.[5]

Again, Frederick Buechner has his marvelous way of expressing this idea of treating ourselves with care: "Love your neighbor as yourself is part of the great commandment. The other way to say it is, Love yourself as your neighbor. Love yourself not in some egocentric, self-serving sense but love yourself the way you would love your friend in the sense of taking care of yourself, nourishing yourself, trying to understand, comfort, strengthen yourself."[6]

Ours can be an exhausting world.

We tend to live lives that over-schedule what *takes* energy and under-schedule what *gives* us energy. To live with spiritual wholeness, to be available compassionately to connect with others, we must do better. We must do what enables resiliency, especially in as stressful a world as ours.

When I speak to groups of ministers, I always like to work into the talk the reminder that the word *pastor* had a nutritional origin shared by the terms *pantry* and *pabulum*. *Pastor* goes back to the word for "pasture"—as in "to pasture the flock"— but before that, its Latin origin is *pateomai*, meaning "I eat."[7]

First, I eat.

Then, and only then, am I ready to feed.

The words of Jesus implore us to fill cups of cold water for those who are thirsty. It is difficult to do if my pitcher is empty.

I have known many caring people—as bright as can be—who forget this balance. They forget to take excellent care of themselves and talk with me of their bewilderment as to why they are exhausted and empty.

Instead, this is what I urge you to do:

Be proactive.
Make room for those you love.
Do the things that give you energy.
Read books that enrich you.
Listen to music that inspires you.
Develop your community.
Get rest.
Pray and meditate daily.
Practice gratitude.
Experience awe.
Laugh often.
Exercise.
Have fun.
Be true to who you are.

Don't wait until fatigue has to remind you.

As Albert Schweitzer put it, "The great secret of success is to go through life as [one] who never gets used up."[8] Having cared for ourselves, we draw from a deeper well as we offer to others. Our giving is out of abundance.

The story is told of tourists on a safari in Africa. They were led on this expedition by natives, who served as their guides and porters. Following the third day, the natives told the tourists they would now stop to rest for a day. The guides told the tourists the issue was not that they were tired but that "we have walked too far too fast and now we must wait for our souls to catch up to us."[9]

We are blessed. And we go out to be a blessing. Sometimes we go too far too fast, and we must pause to be blessed again, to be ready to go out another day.

CHAPTER 14

Compassion and Courage

Be strong, and let your heart take courage,
all you who wait for the LORD.
—Psalm 31:24

Compassion may take us to the deepest places of the human heart, to the tenderest regions of life experience. We engage relationships. Compassion is not what we bring to them but who we are with them.

We enter personally into the hurt, the disappointment, the joy of others. If not, our caring will be of limited value. We open ourselves to an emotional closeness and intimacy.

Henri Nouwen wrote, "No one can help anyone without becoming involved, without entering with his whole person into the painful situation, without taking the risk of becoming hurt, wounded or even destroyed in the process."[1]

If we are willing to open ourselves, our empathy may resonate with another's pain in ways we never had known before. We did not realize a human life could hurt as deeply as the one who is sitting in tears before us. To be intimately in the presence of this pain takes courage. We feel for the person.

The hurt that person feels may get us in touch with old wounds of our own that need attention. We must have the courage to open up any such painful issues from our own personal history and give those memories the care they deserve—making us even more available to join others with theirs.

Courage has been defined as the "mental or moral strength to . . . withstand danger, fear, or difficulty."[2] The "mental or moral strength"—yes, as we have discovered, compassion is a collaboration of the mind and of the heart—is often seen in decisions and courageous acts made in the face of threat and risk. Those choices are formed, fueled, and guided by the heart and the soul to which the mind, in its acts of will, responds.

Courage is often needed to live out our compassion.

The word *courage* comes from the Latin *cor*, meaning "heart," the seat of feeling.[3] Courage always begins with the heart. It requires passion of the heart to overcome the natural hesitation of fear or anxiety. Only then are we able—emboldened by that courage—to choose to speak or act or listen or be who we feel called to be in any given moment.

Ethics and Values

Let's step back for a quick ethics lesson on values.

There are two types of values, and the distinction, I find, is needed to understand the importance of courage.

The two types are *intrinsic* values and *operational* values.

Intrinsic values are those that can be lived out in their own right. Honesty—I tell the truth. Respect—I treat others with the honor they deserve. Intrinsic values include the five core, universal values of respect, responsibility, honesty, fairness, and compassion.

Operational (sometimes called instrumental) values are those values that generate intrinsic values. These include patience, persistence, and courage. These operational values give wings, energy, and motivation to intrinsic values.[4]

My intrinsic value of responsibility may need the operational value of persistence to live it out. My value of respect may need patience to maintain it. And my value of compassion may need courage to propel me, to embolden me to walk into the room of a friend who is living the final days of her life.

As C. S. Lewis put it, "Courage is not simply one of the virtues, but the form of every virtue at the testing point."[5]

I would also add that compassion is the beneficiary of all operational values. Many are the times when patience and persistence are just as needed to motivate and guide the weary and frustrated soul wanting to care in a situation that is difficult.

The Courage to Care

Courage is often needed to live out our compassion.

It is the courage of emotional intimacy. It is the willingness to be vulnerable in opening our hearts, risking what we may feel in response to what is shared and experienced. It is the willingness to step onto the sacred ground and listen to the profound hurt of one who has been betrayed by a spouse or who has buried a child.

To remain open and compassionate in those moments takes nothing less than a spirit of courage.

Then there are those moments when we are confronted with a need for compassion, and a different kind of courage is required.

In a middle school cafeteria a girl is being verbally assaulted with disparaging words that belittle and shame.

Under the heading of "prayer concerns" a Bible study has turned into a gossip session, and a woman's character is being questioned with only a hint of evidence.

In the men's grill at the club the conversation takes an ugly turn and becomes sexist and racist, and all those around the table seem to be in unison, laughing together.

In a high school locker room a young freshman is being bullied and feeling humiliation that could last a lifetime.

Such moments in life call for a kind of compassion that has one standing alone, going against the tide for the love of a person or a race or a gender.

It is not easy, which is why it takes courage.

Stands have to be taken. As persons of integrity and compassion, we cannot do otherwise.

Dr. Robert Coles was driving into New Orleans on his way to a medical meeting one morning in the fall of 1960. Coles was a Harvard-trained psychiatrist, specializing in trauma and stress.

As he drove through New Orleans, traffic came completely to a stop. It was total gridlock. People began getting out of their cars, leaving them in the middle of the street, and walking ahead. Coles did the same thing. He followed the people into a raging mob—screaming, taunting, and threatening as they surrounded the entrance of a school.

Then he saw the focus of the attention.

There was a small black girl, six years old, being escorted by U. S. Marshals through the frenzied crowd and into the William Franz Elementary School. They yelled names at her and threatened to kill her—all in language profane, vile, and hostile. She held her head high, walked into her school, and began the first grade.

She was the epitome of courage.

The little girl was Ruby Bridges. We all remember her, as that moment was captured by Norman Rockwell in one of his most famous paintings he titled "The Problem We All Live With."

She is depicted in her white dress walking into school carrying her books, her ruler, and her pencils, with two Marshals ahead of her and two behind—and the juice from a tomato dripping on the wall behind her as the tomato fell to the sidewalk.

Later, Robert Coles was to gain access to Ruby and her family to learn more from this remarkable girl. He learned of her faith in God that gave her the courage to walk into school each morning through the hostility and chaos.

He had been told by her teacher that one morning, as she was walking toward the school building, she stopped and said something.

He asked Ruby about it, if she was talking to one of the men threatening her. She said, "I wasn't talking to the people . . . I was talking to God . . . I was praying for the people in the street."

He asked, "Why would you pray for those people?"
Her eyes widened, and she asked, "Don't you think
they need praying for?" She continued, "I always say
the same thing. . . . 'Please, dear God, forgive them,
because they do not know what they are doing.' "[6]
The courage of compassion.
Ruby walked to her school with compassion for
her race. She paused in prayer with compassion for all.

Tough Love

The courage to take a stand in the face of risk is one kind of courageous compassion.

Compassion isn't just about
hand-holding.

Still another is the courage to mirror the truth to one who may not want to hear it.

There is a phrase in Ephesians that has always stood out to me. Paul begins one of his teachings with the words, "But speaking the truth in love . . ." (Ephesians 4:15). *Speak the truth in love*—what a perfect balance.

What is to be spoken is the truth. *How* it is to be spoken is with love—with thoughtfulness, sensitivity, and respect.

Speak the truth. The word *true* has its origin in an Old English term that meant "*loyalty*" and "*fidelity.*" The German origin added the concept of "*faithful.*"

Loyalty—fidelity—faithfulness.

There is a loyalty to the relationship and a fidelity to honesty that we honor in faithfully speaking the truth.

In love. The intent, the motivation, behind the speaking of the truth is loving-kindness.

Psychologist Abraham Maslow wrote, "I suppose it is tempting, if the only tool you have is a hammer, to treat everything as if it were a nail."[7] As you have noticed, my main focus in urging compassion is promoting a gentleness of the spirit, because that sensitivity is lacking in a world that needs it. But Maslow is right. Kindness can't be the only tool in the compassionate toolbox.

Sometimes gentle empathy isn't what is needed. It doesn't work for every situation.

Tough love is what they call it. It's what "speaking the truth in love" is often about.

I have a friend who has no problem with doing that. "Greer, only a friend will tell you . . ." he may begin. And he then will tell me—whatever it is—as only a friend will. He is speaking the truth from a truly loving place. It may be pleasant truth. Or it may be disturbing. Yet it is truth I *need* to hear.

Pleasant truth or disturbing truth—my friend comes to the relationship with both tools in the box. And so must we. Compassion isn't just about hand-holding. Sometimes we metaphorically have to grab the lapels and—with intense compassion—get in someone's face with the truth.

Addiction. Alcoholism. Spousal abuse. Infidelity. The list goes on of the tough issues that must be taken head-on. There is nothing warm or fuzzy about confronting these issues. But the compassion behind such courageous conversations is profound.

He was a big, imposing offensive tackle, signed to play for a major college team. He hit the practice field one August morning to begin his college career with all the confidence and talent he needed.

Yet, as gifted as he was athletically, his background left him badly lacking in maturity or any hint of academic interest. He was regularly unprepared for class and soon fell behind academically. Plus, there was a problem with drinking.

The seasoned coaching staff had seen this before. Tough love would be required beyond the practice field. They structured his life so he could benefit from the education his scholarship offered. Study halls were set up and tutors assigned. These were required. No options. No excuses.

Tough love.

In the weeks that followed, he increasingly cut classes, so he ran predawn laps around the field. Graduate assistants escorted him to his buildings for each class . . . only to learn he was walking into each building, straight down the hall, and out the other side.

He had been given every opportunity.

He was called into the office of the head coach. The message was simple: Actions have consequences. We have tried everything and nothing has worked. You will have to get your things and go home.

Tough love doesn't win every time.

Nine years later, Coach was fired. As he was packing up his office, he received a phone call. To his surprise, it was from the talented offensive tackle dismissed from the team almost a decade before. He *paused before taking the call, imagining what he would hear. "I guess what goes around comes around. Can't say I'm upset to hear you got fired, too," was a clear possibility.*

Coach picked up the phone and was greeted with the warmest expression of concern. The young man wanted his former coach to know how saddened he was to hear the news and to thank the one who had sent him packing for all he had done for him.

He wanted Coach to know that nine years ago he had gone home, shaken by the events of what had happened. It got his attention. He regrouped, stopped drinking, went back to school, later married, and was now working hard at a good job and teaching Sunday school.

The former player again expressed his support and concluded, "I thought this might be a good time to give you a call."

Tough love won.

It often does.

CHAPTER 15

Compassion and Character

The law indeed was given through Moses.
—John 1:17a

The journey toward full compassion, for most, is launched with the decision to carve out a life with values, a life of character. Subconsciously, the stage may have been set by engaging loving relationships in childhood, but our cognitive understanding emerges with the intentional development of character. Parents and teachers guide us in making the first steps in the process of learning how to care. It begins with life lessons in respect, kindness, and thoughtfulness—essentially, the foundation of the Golden Rule.

I have known many collectors over the years. Some have collections of art or first edition books. Others prefer wine or rare coins.
  I was talking with an appraiser once who had been called to a man's home to appraise his collection of antique firearms. After an initial evaluation, he told his client he had bad news for him. "What you have isn't really a collection. It's an accumulation."

An accumulation.

The man asked the appraiser the inevitable question, "What's the difference between the two?"

"A collection," the expert explained, "is put together intentionally, with purpose and thought."

Often in response to decisions with which life confronts them, young people decide who they are and what they believe.

Lives of character are put together intentionally, with purpose and thought.

Through our childhoods we accumulated values. This accumulation is from those principles, philosophies, and attitudes we picked up here and there. It includes those we learned in our childhood homes, those underscored by our communities, those taught and those modeled, and some we came up with on our own.

It is an accumulation, a rather random hodgepodge of attitudes and principles gathered from the world around us.

From it, if we are thoughtful and wise, we begin to discern. If we want a true *collection* of values, we begin with our accumulations. We reflect. We evaluate. We sort out. We keep, and we discard. We do it thoughtfully and intentionally. We look to the teachings of our faith. We read what wise minds have written. We listen to those we respect.

We carefully sift through and handpick our values. We choose them, intentionally.

Simply put, the quality of our lives will be based, in part, on the excellence of this process of selection. Each significant decision we make is based, consciously or subconsciously, on the values and attitudes that serve as our foundation.

A life of character begins with the integration of those values we have chosen.

I was a child in the 1950s. It was from that era, growing up in a small southern town, that I gathered my pool of principles and values. A number of them were from my father, who was a remarkable man. He loved children and wondered how he could make the world a better place for them.

I wandered downtown one summer afternoon with a freedom we children had in that era—unheard of today. I stopped in to see my dad and was talking with his receptionist when I heard him call to me from down the hall.

I walked back and stepped into his office. There sat an African American man. He stood as I walked in, and as he extended his hand, Dad said to me, "Here is someone I want you to meet." We shook hands and introductions were made. We made small talk about my summer baseball team.

There was then the inevitable pause in the conversation, and as accurately as I can recall, the man asked me, "Do you know what I'm doing here?"

"No, sir, I don't."

"Well, you white folks have a public swimming pool to enjoy in the summer. But on the colored side of town our kids have to swim in whatever lakes or ponds they can find. Your daddy doesn't think that's right. He is working to see if we can find a way to get a pool built for our children."

Life experience offers us the values we later choose for our collections. As childhood gives way to adolescence, young women and men make their selections and put their stamps on their lives.

They stand for something.

Often in response to decisions with which life confronts them, they decide who they are and what they believe. They become grounded. It is seen in their countenance, in their confidence. Not arrogance. Not grandiosity. Confidence—in who they are, in that for which they stand, and in how they then go about their lives.

They have purpose.

I am reminded of the way a colleague in ministry once put it: "Most days I prefer the language of 'purpose' to 'mission statement,' because most mission statements sound like they should just be written on letterhead rather than etched upon the human heart."[1]

As we mature emotionally and faithfully, we become collectors—*with intentionality*—of the finest values. We decide which are worthy. This gives us direction and purpose.

> *Persons of character develop a life of values by beginning as an ordinary piece of cloth. Into the fabric they weave elegant, vibrant threads to form the tapestry of their lives. These threads are the values they have chosen and made into their virtues.*
>
> *The word ordinary is important here. The origin of the word is "positive." It had nothing to do with mediocrity. It was from the weaving industry, and a fabric that was ordinary was one with order. It was appropriately consistent. The first yard of a bolt of cloth was virtually identical to the last.*

Next, weavers would weave threads of royal blue and crimson red and gold into the fabric. As the threads were added, the cloth became a beautiful tapestry. A new word then came into being. The prefix extra was merged with ordinem, which became our English word extraordinary.[2]

To build a tapestry of character, imagine each thread as a virtue woven into the fabric of ordinary lives. The royal blue, let's say, is respect. The crimson red is honesty. The gold is compassion . . . and on through the list of attributes we esteem and hold in highest regard.

Day by day, with threads in hand, persons of character will weave. They focus intuitively on incorporating the finest into the routine of our lives.

We look at them in awe at what a magnificent tapestry their lives have become!

Most of us intuitively turn to our faith first as the best source of relational values. It points us to those worthy of priority.

Compassion emerges as the virtue of prominence.

Hear the poetic beauty in these words from the Scriptures, "Whatever is true, whatever is honorable, whatever is just, whatever is pure, whatever is pleasing, whatever is commendable, if there is any excellence and if there is anything worthy of praise, think about these things" (Philippians 4:8).

It has always intrigued me that, as much as religions and societies around the world may differ, the values they emphasize parallel each other with remarkable similarity.

Humankind seems to be hardwired for moral living. Paul wrote, "They show that what the law requires is written on their hearts, to which their own conscience also bears witness" (Romans 2:15). The predisposition for morality seems to have already been in our hearts. Perhaps it is from that spark, the image of God, with which we all are created. Those universal values common to cultures worldwide include

> respect,
>> responsibility,
>>> compassion,
>>>> honesty, and
>>>>> fairness.[3]

Each of these values is at the core of the Christian faith.

Each is worthy of priority—of our attention and focus. Each enriches us and makes us finer persons. Each becomes a part of who we are.

Yet one of these values tends to emerge. For persons of faith, *compassion emerges as the virtue of prominence.* As we are grounded in all of the worthy values, compassion continues to surface as the one at the center of our focus. Perhaps the others—respect, responsibility, honesty, and fairness—are more readily accessed, becoming givens earlier in our development, and truly to live with compassion requires more maturity and intentionality.

More likely, compassion emerges as the virtue claiming our attention because it is foundationally at the heart of the life and the message of Jesus. He taught it, just as he lived it.

The clearest picture of God is, indeed, the life of Jesus of Nazareth, a window into the soul and heart of the divine. What he consistently lived was the epitome of compassion, as he put his hands on the leper no one else would touch or called the most despised man in town out of the tree so he could have dinner with him.

What he taught was the same message, leaving us with the engraved image in our minds of the Samaritan kneeling at the side of the wounded Jew, doing all he could to help.

Time after time in the Gospels, the writers, using identical wording, would describe a scene in the life of Jesus and preface his response with, "and he had compassion for them." The account that would follow showed him responding with heartfelt caring to the need or hurt. He was moved, and he responded.

Compassion was the spontaneous reaction Jesus had when he saw distress, struggle, or hardship.

This compassion, for most of us, becomes a cornerstone we lay early in developing the foundation of our character. It begins as a value. It is taught and learned along with the others. We had been loved, so we knew from life experience that to care was a good thing, but we showed compassion early on because we were so trained. With intentional focus and practice it becomes a habitual part of our lifestyles. We engrave it into our living as one of our virtues.

This is a healthy beginning.

Laying a cornerstone is always an important step, but it is only a beginning. The construction is initiated and then continues. At this early stage of development our compassion comes from the mind, from the wise decision for character. It comes from an important place but not yet with a motivation from our greatest depth. In fact, our focus is more on our actions, on *what we do* than it is on *why we do it*. We are caring because we *learned to care*. This is not superficial. It is simply where we were earlier in our journeys. We are developing. We are young and working diligently to do what is right. We have been taught to have compassion, and we are living it out.

"The law indeed was given through Moses; grace and truth came through Jesus Christ" (John 1:17). We tend to begin with "the law," with the behavioral rights and wrongs, with the dos and don'ts.

As time passes, however, we mature in our faith and our understanding of who we are in the world. How we live out our lives shifts from what we *should* do to what we *want* to do—even feel *called* to do—because it has become a natural expression of who we are.

I had written an earlier book on integrity and have enjoyed many conversations on the topic since then. I have heard several say, in various ways, "But I already have integrity. I do the right thing." We then engage in rich conversations about *why* we do the right thing.

In order to fully develop ourselves, we need to know *why* we are honoring the values we chose. Some reasons are more grounded, more anchored than others.

For many it's to stay out of trouble—which is good. It keeps stores from being robbed and red lights from being run. But it is not a reason of high calling.

For others, it's to look good. To be seen doing the honorable thing is excellent public relations and socially advantageous. Again, it's not a bad thing, but it is chiefly self-serving. Jesus was less than impressed, saying something about the hypocrites already having received their reward.

Developing our moral and spiritual lives is an ever-deepening process. We learn. We grow. We experience. We grow from the experience.

"The law indeed was given," and we are thankful for it. It keeps social order and gives aid to those in need. Yet when we respond to "the law" we are responding to authority.

When we respond to grace, we respond from the heart and soul touched by the love of God.

CHAPTER 16

Compassion from Deeper Places

Grace and truth came through Jesus Christ.
—John 1:17b

Compassion, we have noted, was chosen by most of us as a part of our character as we emerged from childhood. We intuitively decided to be kind and caring. It was something we did.

Yet *seasoned* compassion comes from a journey that has taken us to deeper places. It clearly includes doing good, but it is not merely about the deeds.

Compassion goes from a *value* to a *virtue* to a *way of being.*

It comes not only from the mind and the heart but ultimately from the soul. Compassion involves a *spiritual maturity,* allowing the good we do to come from a place filled with grace and gratitude. Over time we intuitively move from doing acts of compassion to being compassionate. The maturation goes from our *acts* to our *attitude* to *who we are.*

In developing lives of compassion we are moving, as the Scriptures say, "from strength to strength" (Psalm 84:7). Or we might paraphrase, "from depth to depth."

It was Music Sunday at church. The sermon was a brief meditation, in order to give all our choirs plenty of time. We were inspired as we heard them—the children's choirs, the youth, and the Chancel Choir.

As the service built to its finale, all the choirs returned to the chancel area. There were the tiers of children down front, with the taller youth behind them, and the adults in the choir loft as they all joined in singing, "He's Got the Whole World in His Hands."

I looked up and down, at each tier of choirs, as they sang. I listened to their words, "He's got all of us here in His hands, He's got all of us here . . ." I heard not only the beauty of their voices but saw the conviction in their faces of the truth in what they were singing. They each showed a confidence in a God who graciously embraces each of us and all of us.

Slowly I looked up and down again, at each of the choirs, and remembered being at each of those stages of life.

Childhood.
Youth.
Adulthood.

Each level had an understanding and theology of the God who held us in his hands, but each was a different level of maturity of understanding.

One was not better than the other. They were simply different. Some had the advantage of childhood— "Unless you change and become like children"— others the wisdom of seasons lived, and each appropriate for where they were.

As I continued listening to that marvelous anthem, I became aware of the harmony of it all. It was not just the beauty of the blending of their voices but the harmony of their ages and places in life. As the choir thrived on the merging of voices, I watched the faces of each age affirming its faith in a God for all ages.

The process of maturing into lives of character was well outlined by Lawrence Kohlberg in *The Psychology of Moral Development*.[1] He describes three levels of moral development with two stages at each level. The first two stages of leading moral lives are about taking care of ourselves—to avoid punishment and to get what we want.

As we mature, we move up to a higher level of wanting to be responsive to other's expectations as we live out our relational roles. Having achieved these, we aspire to being responsible members of our broader society. The top pair on Kohlberg's scale is the desire to live in accordance with the rightness of society's standards and, finally, to live out our own values we have claimed to be true for ourselves.

Compassion is usually introduced to us as a core value as we develop our lives of character. More, much more, will be revealed to us about compassion as we continue to grow. Its motivation, its source, and even its passion, will shift to spring more deeply, from the heart, and finally the soul.

The Spiritual Ascent

I recently parked in the parking deck of a large office building in our city. The elevator took me up several levels of the parking deck to the first floor of offices. I got off there and walked down the hall to another bank of elevators that would take me to the floor for my meeting.

Later it occurred to me—this is a metaphor for growing into our most compassionate selves. Kohlberg's levels of moral development took us from earliest childhood up the first six stories, to where we each claimed compassion as a central value of our character.

Those are our moral elevators.

It is another bank of elevators, those down the hall, with which we make our spiritual ascent.

As Kohlberg guided us through our moral growth, we turn to our theological sherpas who guide us through the growth of our spiritual selves—though we know that in life our moral and spiritual maturity intertwine and overlap.

James Fowler is one of those guides as he describes his detailed *Stages of Faith* through the life cycle.[2] Richard Rohr is another, as he is equally helpful in walking us through the spiritual development of the two halves of our lives.[3] And then there are the reflections of E. F. Schumacher who uses the biblical Hebrew outline of Law, Prophets, and Wisdom to parallel our journey through structure to critique to maturity.[4]

Yet the description with which I resonate most clearly when I think of this spiritual ascent is that of Ken Wilber.[5] He writes of spiritual maturity from

> *belief,*
>> to *faith,*
>>> to *direct experience*, and, finally, to what he refers to as
>>>> *permanent adaptation.*

I step onto this elevator at the level of *belief.*

This floor is cognitive, of the mind. The focus is on symbols and concepts. Belief is about understanding and conceptualizing the tenets of the faith. It doesn't have to do with actual spiritual experience, yet it holds the foundation to help us achieve it.

After a time, belief alone loses its appeal. It is a set of ideas and theology with no spiritual life and energy of its own. It is merely thoughts about God's relationship with the world—but with no actual experience of a relationship with God.

It is when we live out God's image within us that we begin to grow into God's likeness.

The next step toward that direct relationship is the transitional stage of *faith*. It begins with the intuition that there is more to spiritual living than just a set of beliefs. As Wilber puts it, "Faith soldiers on when belief becomes unbelievable, for faith hears the faint but direct calling of a higher reality . . . that, being beyond the mind is *beyond belief*."[6]

Faith leads us then to the *direct experience* of the presence of God. On this level we become aware of the spiritual presence of the divine in our midst. It may be a mountaintop or peak experience. For others, it's during meditation or contemplative prayer that God's presence is felt as a quiet, dawning awareness where the peaks may extend into plateaus.

As our spiritual awareness rises, some may come to know a *permanent adaptation* or a consistent connection with the holy in their midst.

The *peak* moments become *plateau* experiences, which can become *a way of life*. The evolution of this awareness can happen only when we are intentional and give significant attention to our spiritual development.

Compassion and Spirituality

I realize in the brevity of this description I may be making the evolution of our moral and spiritual lives seem far too neat and tidy.

It is not.

These are simply the basics, the phases of how we tend to mature in our faith. There are always fits and starts. We move forward just in time to slip back into old patterns.

If we are intentional, this development of spiritual maturity becomes our journey. A spiritual life is an ascent not quickly achieved. It is an evolving process that takes its time.

We live increasingly out of "the Christ in you," as Paul phrased it, the spark of the divine.

Though I have known profoundly loving people at every level of faith development, the more personally we connect with the sacred dimension of life, the more we are likely to feel its grace. As we become more spiritual, we inch ever closer to the God who created grace and defined compassion. The deeper we go, the more clearly we see through God's eyes.

Remember the distinction we made in our moral thinking between *values* and *virtues*? Our values are what we *believe*. Our virtues are what we *live*.

In our spiritual lives there is a parallel to this in our being created in the *image* of God and our growing into God's *likeness*.[7] The image of God is the blessing with which we are born. It is the spark of the divine, God's own grace within our spiritual DNA.

It is a gift, inherited at our creation. This image of God within us may be realized or not, actualized or dormant.

It is when we live out God's image within us that we begin to grow into God's likeness.

What was potential is brought to life as we claim the image of grace, of love, of compassion that was always there. As we increasingly, consistently live out that image we become more grace-filled and more gracious. We mature; we grow into that divine likeness.

Think of those persons you have known who embody spiritual depth. See how they relate. Listen to their voices. Look into their eyes. There is something different. There is something about the spirit of those rare few. You've seen it, haven't you? They relate from that deeper place. They speak from the soul. You hear it in their voices, and you see it in their eyes.

It has been said, "You do not have a soul. You are a soul. You have a body."

We are souls. We are spiritual beings at our core. We honor that by living, as best we can, from that center, from the image of God with which we are created.

As we live from our spiritual core we tap into a wellspring of care and compassion we had never known before. We feel sympathy, a personal caring at others' pain; but it is much more than sympathy. We feel empathy as we hurt with them; but it is even more than empathy. We feel compassion. We *must* respond.

To live with compassion because it is a part of a life of character is to live with integrity—which is a wonderful thing and the foundation for what follows. To be compassionate because "I cannot not do it," because I feel the surge, the passion of "doing no other" comes from an even *more* sustaining place.

Charlie Roberts was the young man who, in a moment of insanity, went to the Amish school and killed five children, wounding five others before killing himself. Charlie's mother, Terri, was driving to his house as she heard the report of the mass killings on the car radio. As she pulled into his driveway, she saw her husband and a state trooper standing there. She got out of the car, and her husband said, "It was Charlie." Then he added, "I'll never face my Amish neighbors again."

Charlie's funeral was a small, private service five days later. The family gathered for the interment at the cemetery. There they saw about forty of their Amish neighbors walking up to join them, "surrounding them like a crescent."

Terri later said, "Love just emanated from them." The family and the Amish prayed and buried Charlie together.

Fast forward ten years. Terri Roberts has a special stop she makes one day each week a decade later. She goes by to see Rosanna. Now fifteen, Rosanna was one of the five-year-old girls shot that day at school. She was shot in the head. Rosanna is tube-fed, in a wheelchair, and has seizures—especially when the anniversary date nears.

One day each week Terri goes to Rosanna's home. She reads to her. She bathes her. She dries her hair. One of the fathers said, "None of us would have ever chosen this. But the relationships that we have built through it, you can't put a price on that."[8]

"You shall love the Lord your God with all your heart, and with all your soul, and with all your mind. . . . You shall love your neighbor as yourself" (Matthew 22:37, 39).

The Amish surrounded them like a crescent. And now Terri goes by once a week and reads to Rosanna, bathes her, and dries her hair.

This is faithful living at its finest. We forgive. We come together. We go forward as one.

It's called compassion.

Epilogue

"Pretend we're dancing." I think back to that marvelous story from the first chapter of this writing.

I am married to as naturally talented a dancer as anyone I know. Her partner is not similarly blessed.

Prior to each of our children's weddings I have not been shy in the number of dance lessons I have taken, knowing how publicly my skills would be on display.

I'm not talented, but I am coachable. I can learn the steps. Yet I would joke with Karen and my instructor that every time I step onto the dance floor I *pretend I'm dancing*.

As we have discussed over these many pages our compassion *is* a dance. We care. There are those who are struggling, and they matter to us.

We invite them to the dance. We step onto the dance floor together. We listen for the music of their hearts. We follow their lead.

The steps are made with empathy and grace.

I can't dance well. But, like you, I can connect with love. On that dance floor, in those relationships, we are not pretending.

And loving compassion, after all, is our dance.

Notes

1. Pretend We're Dancing

1. Eric Partridge, *Origins: A Short Etymological Dictionary of Modern English* (New York: Macmillan, 1966), 475.

2. Partridge, *Origins*, 475.

3. Partridge, *Origins*, 638.

4. Partridge, *Origins*, 475.

5. Partridge, *Origins*, 475.

6. Carl Rogers, *The Carl Rogers Reader*, ed. Howard Kirschenbaum and Valerie Land Henderson (New York: Houghton Mifflin Harcourt, 1989), 226.

7. Thomas Keating, "Seekers of Ultimate Mystery," Awakin.org, January 9, 2012, www.awakin.org/read/view.php?tid=766.

8. *Merriam-Webster's Collegiate Dictionary*, 11th ed., s.v. "compassion" (Springfield, MA, 2005), 253.

9. Frederick Buechner, *Wishful Thinking* (New York: Harper & Row, 1969), 15.

10. Matthew Fox, *Original Blessing: A Primer in Creation Spirituality Presented in Four Paths, Twenty-Six Themes, and Two Questions* (New York: Jeremy P. Tarcher/Putnam, 1983).

2. To Look from the Heart

1. Frederick Buechner, *Whistling in the Dark* (New York: HarperCollins, 1988), 17.

3. To Feel from the Heart

1. Susan Stamberg, "Vermeer's 'Woman in Blue' Brings Her Mystery, Allure to L.A.," National Public Radio, March 1, 2013; www .npr.org/2013/03/01/172899519/vermeers-woman-in-blue-brings-her -mystery-allure-to-l-a.

2. M. Craig Barnes, "I Don't Feel Your Pain," *Christian Century* (July 23, 2014): 35.

3. Rachel Corbett, *You Must Change Your Life: The Story of Rainer Maria Rilke and Auguste Rodin* (New York: W. W. Norton and Company, 2016), 21–22.

4. Marc Ian Barasch, *The Compassionate Life: Walking the Path of Kindness* (San Francisco: Berrett-Koehler, 2009), 30.

5. Corbett, *You Must Change Your Life*, 22.

6. Dale Ahlquist, "Lecture 91: The Boat on a Stormy Sea," The American Chesterton Society, www.chesterton.org/lecture-91/.

7. Harold Holzer, "A Common Bond of Grief," *The Wall Street Journal*, February 12, 2016, www.wsj.com/articles/a-common-bond-of -grief-1455312276.

4. To Listen for the Heart

1. David Augsburger, *Caring Enough to Hear and Be Heard* (Ventura, CA: Regal, 1982), 12.

2. Simone Weil, *Correspondence* (Lausanne: Editions l'Aged'Homme, 1982), 18, as found on www.quora.com/What-is-the-exact-source-and -citation-for-the-Simone-Weil-quotation-%E2%80%9CAttention -is-the-rarest-and-purest-form-of-generosity.

3. Mary Pipher, "Fostering the Moral Imagination," *Psychotherapy Networker* (January–February 2007): 50–51.

4. Michael Moore et al., *Bowling for Columbine* (USA: MGM Home Entertainment, 2003).

5. Seth S. Horowitz, "The Science and Art of Listening," *The New York Times* (November 9, 2012).

6. E. E. Cummings as quoted on My Soul in Silence Waits (blog), February 25, 2015, "The True Self," https://insilencewaits.wordpress.com/tag/thomas-merton/.

7. James Hillman, *Insearch* (Irving, TX: Spring Publications, 1967), 31.

8. Stephen R. Covey, *The Seven Habits of Highly Effective People: Restoring the Character Ethic* (New York: Simon & Schuster, 1989), 239.

9. Atul Gawande, *Being Mortal: Medicine and What Matters in the End* (New York: Metropolitan Books, 2014), 198.

5. The Spirit of Compassion

1. George Saunders, *Congratulations, by the Way: Some Thoughts on Kindness* (New York: Random House, 2014).

2. Susan M. Pollak, Thomas Pedulla, and Ronald D. Siegel, *Sitting Together: Essential Skills for Mindfulness-Based Psychotherapy* (New York: Guilford, 2014), 29–30.

3. Paul Kalanithi, *When Breath Becomes Air* (New York: Random House, 2016), 81.

4. Henri J. M. Nouwen, *Out of Solitude: Three Meditations on the Christian Life* (Notre Dame, IN: Ave Maria, 1974), 34.

5. Robert Coles, *Lives of Moral Leadership: Men and Women Who Have Made a Difference* (New York: Random House, 2000), 34–35.

6. Eric Partridge, *Origins: A Short Etymological Dictionary of Modern English* (New York: Macmillan, 1966), 475.

7. Anthony de Mello, *One Minute Wisdom* (New York: Doubleday, 1988), 4.

8. Catherine of Siena, *The Dialogue of St. Catherine of Siena* (Vancouver: Eremitical Press, 2009), 10.

9. Richard Rohr, *Things Hidden: Scripture as Spirituality* (Cincinnati: Franciscan Media, 2008), 28.

6. The Gift of Grace

1. My thanks to Philip Yancey for the inspiration of this listing from his book *What's So Amazing About Grace?* (Grand Rapids, MI: Zondervan, 1997).

2. Frederick Buechner, *Wishful Thinking* (New York: Harper & Row, 1969), 33.

3. Yancey, *What's So Amazing About Grace?* 12.

4. Eric Partridge, *Origins: A Short Etymological Dictionary of Modern English* (New York: Macmillan, 1966), 262.

5. *Shorter Oxford English Dictionary on Historical Principles*, 6th ed., vol. 1, *s.v.* "grace" (Oxford, UK: Oxford University Press, 2007).

6. *Merriam-Webster's Collegiate Dictionary*, 11th ed., *s.v.* "grace" (Springfield, MA, 2005).

7. Alvin Sugarman, e-mail with the author, October 9, 2017.

7. The Grace of the Still Small Voice

1. Maria Popova, "Leonard Cohen on Creativity, Hard Work, and Why You Should Never Quit Before You Know What It Is You're Quitting," Brain Pickings, July 15, 2014, www.brainpickings. org/2014/07/15/leonard-cohen-paul-zollo-creativity/.

2. Coleman Barks, *The Essential Rumi* (New York: HarperCollins, 2004), 36.

3. Richard Rohr, "The Duty of the Present Moment," Richard Rohr's Daily Meditation, December 7, 2014, http://myemail.constant contact.com/Richard-Rohr-s-Meditation--The-Duty-of-the-Present -Moment.html?soid=1103098668616&aid=FFiE61nKWH4.

4. Helen Keller, *The Story of My Life* (New York: W. W. Norton, 2003), 398.

5. Keller, *Story of My Life*, 27–28.

6. John Michael Talbot and Steve Rabey, *The Lessons of St. Francis* (New York: Penguin Group, 1998), 210–11.

8. Never Beyond the Reach of God's Grace

1. Frederick Buechner, *Secrets in the Dark: A Life in Sermons* (New York: HarperCollins, 2006), 51.

2. Barbara Brown Taylor, *Learning to Walk in the Dark* (New York: HarperCollins, 2014).

3. Gerald G. May, *The Dark Night of the Soul: A Psychiatrist Explores the Connection Between Darkness and Spiritual Growth* (New York: HarperCollins, 2004), 3.

4. Peter Applebome, "Loss of Speech Evokes the Voice of a Writer," *New York Times* (March 7, 2011).

5. Naomi Shihab Nye, *Words Under the Words: Selected Poems* (Portland, OR: Far Corner, 1980), 42.

6. Richard Rohr, *Eager to Love: The Alternative Way of Francis of Assisi* (Cincinnati: Franciscan Media, 2014), 19.

9. Our Response to Grace

1. F. Forrester Church, ed., *The Essential Tillich: An Anthology of the Writings of Paul Tillich* (Chicago: University of Chicago Press, 1987), 201.

2. David Brooks, "The Structure of Gratitude," *New York Times* (July 28, 2015).

3. Adrian Baschuk, "California Fires Nearly Contained," CNN Live at Daybreak, November 3, 2003, television broadcast, https://travel.cnn.com/TRANSCRIPTS/0311/03/lad.03.html.

4. Karl Barth as quoted in Helmut Gollwitzer, *An Introduction to Protestant Theology*, trans. David Cairns (Louisville: Westminster John Knox, 1982), 174.

10. Standing Before Your Burning Bush

1. Jean-Pierre de Caussade, *Abandonment to Divine Providence*, trans. John Beevers (New York: Image Books, 2014), 18.

2. Charles Dickens, *David Copperfield* (New York: Dodd, Mead, 1984), 1.

11. Compassion and Service

1. Albert Schweitzer, "Who Is Albert Schweitzer," Albert Schweitzer's Leadership for Life, http://aschweitzer.com/abouta.html.

12. Compassion and Boundaries

1. Henry Cloud and John Townsend, *Boundaries: When to Say Yes, How to Say No—to Take Control of Your Life* (Grand Rapids, MI: Zondervan, 1992), 86.

2. Robert D. Lupton, *Toxic Charity: How Churches and Charities Hurt Those They Help (And How to Reverse It)* (New York: HarperCollins, 2011), 15, 34.

3. Lupton, *Toxic Charity*, 53.

13. Compassion Toward Ourselves

1. Frederick Buechner, *Telling Secrets* (New York: HarperCollins, 1991), 28.

2. Kristin Neff, "The Science of Self-Compassion," in *Wisdom and Compassion in Psychotherapy: Deepening Mindfulness in Clinical Practice*, ed. Christopher K. Germer and Ronald D. Siegel (New York: Guilford Press, 2012), 87–88. Also, Kristin Neff, *Self-Compassion: The Proven Power of Being Kind to Yourself* (New York: HarperCollins, 2011), 8.

3. Neff, *Self-Compassion*, 27.

4. Neff, *Self-Compassion*, 88.

5. Neff, *Self-Compassion*, 80–81.

6. Buechner, *Telling Secrets*, 27.

7. Eric Partridge, *Origins: A Short Etymological Dictionary of Modern English* (New York: Macmillan, 1966), 474.

8. Albert Schweitzer, *Memoirs of Childhood and Youth*, trans. C. T. Campion (Whitefish, MT: Kessinger, 2010).

9. Harold Kushner, *The Lord Is My Shepherd: Healing Wisdom of the Twenty-Third Psalm* (New York: Anchor, 2004), 60.

14. Compassion and Courage

1. Henri J. M. Nouwen, *The Wounded Healer: Ministry in Contemporary Society* (New York: Doubleday, 1979), 72.

2. *Merriam-Webster's Collegiate Dictionary*, 11th ed., *s.v.* "courage" (Springfield, MA, 2005), 287.

3. Eric Partridge, *Origins: A Short Etymological Dictionary of Modern English* (New York: Macmillan, 1966), 120.

4. Rushworth Kidder, *Moral Courage* (New York: HarperCollins, 2005), 68–69.

5. C. S. Lewis, *Screwtape Letters: Annotated Edition* (New York: HarperCollins, 1942), 174.

6. "Robert Coles on Ruby Bridges," An interview with Robert Coles, YouTube, www.youtube.com/watch?v=XPK3zQM2dHU.

7. Abraham H. Maslow, *The Psychology of Science: A Reconnaissance* (New York: Harper & Row, 1966), 15–16.

15. Compassion and Character

1. Dalton Rushing, "Living on Purpose," *Monday Morning in North Georgia*, an online publication of the North Georgia Conference of the United Methodist Church, October 21, 2012, http://northga-email.brtapp.com/viewarchive/928.

2. Eric Partridge, *Origins: A Short Etymological Dictionary of Modern English* (New York: Macmillan, 1966), 456.

3. Rushworth Kidder, *Moral Courage* (New York: HarperCollins, 2005), 10, 46–47, 50.

16. Compassion from Deeper Places

1. Lawrence Kohlberg, *The Psychology of Moral Development: The Nature and Validity of Moral Stages*, vol. 2 of Essays on Moral Development series (San Francisco: Harper & Row, 1984), 174–76.

2. James W. Fowler, *Stages of Faith: The Psychology of Development and the Quest for Meaning* (New York: HarperCollins, 1981).

3. Richard Rohr, *Falling Upward: A Spirituality for the Two Halves of Life* (San Francisco: Jossey-Bass, 2011).

4. E. F. Schumacher, *A Guide for the Perplexed* (New York: HarperCollins, 1977).

5. Ken Wilber, *The Essential Ken Wilber: An Introductory Reader* (Boston: Shambhala, 1998), 176–84.

6. Wilber, *Essential Ken Wilber*, 178.

7. Richard Rohr, *Silent Compassion: Finding God in Contemplation* (Cincinnati: Franciscan Media, 2014), 46–47.

8. "A Decade After Amish School Shooting, Gunman's Mother Talks of Forgiveness," Story Corps, National Public Radio, September 30, 2016, www.npr.org/2016/09/30/495905609/a-decade-after-amish -school-shooting-gunman-s-mother-talks-of-forgiveness.

Read More From Ronald J. Greer

Now That They Are Grown: Successfully Parenting Your Adult Children

ISBN: 9781426741913

Make a smooth transition from parenting children to being parents of young adults. Discover ways to nurture your adult children while encouraging their independence and maturity. You'll learn how to have balance, respond to their struggles, be supportive yet not intrusive, and be caring without enabling dependency.

If You Know Who You Are, You Will Know What to Do: Living with Integrity

ISBN: 9781426744617

Take an in-depth look at what integrity is and how to apply it to daily life, by exploring the two sides of integrity: personal integrity and moral integrity.

Markings on the Windowsill: A Book About Grief That's Really About Hope

ISBN: 9780687333639

Experience a moving book that draws on the author's experiences as a father and pastoral counselor to offer hope, help, and healing to people who are grieving.

Find Additional Information and Other Books to Enjoy at AbingdonPress.com

Abingdon Press
Growing in Life, Serving in Faith